THE
Voice of the Soul

THE
Voice of the Soul

Katherine Tingley

Commonwealth Book Company
St. Martin, Ohio

Copyright © 1928 by Katherine Tingley.
Originally published by The Aryan Theosophical Press for the
Woman's International Theosophical League in 1928.
Copyright © 2023 by Commonwealth Book Company, Inc.

All rights reserved. No part of this book may be reproduced in any form or by any means without the prior written consent of the publisher, excepting brief quotes used in reviews. Printed in the United States of America.

ISBN: 978-1-948986-55-7

FRONTISPIECE (FROM THE ORIGINAL):

THE OPEN-AIR GREEK THEATER
INTERNATIONAL THEOSOPHICAL HEADQUARTERS
POINT LOMA, CALIFORNIA

The first in America, built in 1901. The Theater has been called "a jewel on the brow of beauty." Its acoustics are perfect, and it has been proclaimed by world-travelers to be the most beautiful Greek Theater in the world.

Dedicated to the
Great Orphan, Humanity

THEOSOPHY is the very spirit of true Religion; and if man's body is kept clean and strong and healthy, and the mind is rightly trained, and the soul is free to grow and aspire, Theosophy will fill the life naturally.

CONTENTS

Section I

THE VOICE OF THE SOUL

The Soul is the Real Man	3
A Child's Spiritual Heritage	5
Imagination, a Divine Attribute of the Soul	9
The Challenge of the Soul	11
The Courage and Joy of the Soul	13
Theosophy the Key	15
Theosophy and Criminology	17
Redemption and the Voice of the Soul	19
The Natural Path to Wisdom	21
The Training of Children	25
Self-Directed Evolution	29
Beware of Counterfeit Theosophy	30
Man Religious by Nature	32
The Optimism of Theosophy	35
Man's Essential Divinity	37
Childhood Impressions	39
The Search for the Soul	44
Now is the Time	47
The Great Impediments to Spiritual Progress	50
The Beauty of a Perfect Life	54
The Eternal Fulfilment of the Law	56
Soul-Power	57

The Value of Life and the Soul's Opportunities ... 58
Inner Illumination 61
The Kingdom of Heaven Within 64
Life a Superb Challenge 67
"Born in Sin" vs. Soul-Courage 71
Warfare and Brotherhood 74
Setting our own Houses in Order 75
Self-Knowledge and Common Sense 77
Râja-Yoga 81

Section II

Helena Petrovna Blavatsky: A Brief Sketch of her Life and of her Mission

A Russian Noblewoman of Marvelous Spiritual Power 87
"The Greatest Spirit of the Nineteenth Century" 88
H. P. Blavatsky and W. Q. Judge 89
H. P. Blavatsky's Childhood 92
Her Spiritual Awakening 94
She Comes to America 95
Founding of the Theosophical Society 98
Her Message 99
The Spreading of Theosophy 102
Man's Essential Divinity 103
Reincarnation 106
"Touching the Fringe of Truth" 108
The Appeal of Theosophy 109

CONTENTS xi

SECTION III

AN INCIDENT OF THE FIRST THEOSOPHICAL WORLD-
TOUR, 1896-7: A STRIKING PROOF OF
REINCARNATION

Meeting with the President of the Khedive's
Tribunal 118
Rameses the Second's Tomb Discovered 120
Egypt's Great King Honored by Modern Beduins
with Ancient Rites 127
Egypt Older than India, America Older than
Either 132
The Promise of Reincarnation 133
Crime and its Prevention 134
Another Chance for All 138
Reincarnation brings Enlightenment 139

SECTION IV

THE PERFECTIBILITY OF MAN

The Preciousness of the Moment 147
Proof of the Perfectibility of Man ......˙... 149
My Meeting with the Teacher 151
The Illumination and Force of the Teacher's
Presence 155
The Challenge of Theosophy 159
The Consciousness of the Soul-life 163
Real and Counterfeit Theosophy 166

CONTENTS

SECTION V

THE INTERNATIONAL THEOSOPHICAL HEADQUARTERS
  The International Theosophical Headquarters,
    Point Loma, San Diego, California 171
  The Spirit of Lomaland 182

SECTION VI

THE THEOSOPHICAL CONCEPTION OF LAW AND ORDER
  Theosophy the Enlightener 195
  Theosophy Offers Truth 198
  No Harsh Remedies 201
  The Hickman Case 204

SECTION VII

THE DRAMA
  "The Eumenides," April, 1927 217

SECTION VIII

THE NEW DAY — EASTER, 1928
  Easter 225
  Resurrect the Divine in Man 231
  Theosophy and Christianity 233
  A Day of Challenge 235
  Nature's Response 239
  Knowledge of Theosophy Essential 243
  The New Day 246

Section IX

UNIVERSAL BROTHERHOOD

Salutations to All the People of the World 249
A New-Year's Message to the Resident-Members
   and Students at the World's Theosophical
   Center, Point Loma, California 250
Universal Brotherhood 253
A New Quality of Optimism Needed 255
Black Marks on America's History 257
No Self-Deception 260
The Place of Reason 262
Human Duality 264

Section X

HERE AND THERE

On Lomaland's Perennial Charms 269
On "Mothers' Day" 272
On White Lotus Day 276
On Optimism 279
On the Immortality of Genius 284
On "The Life of Pythagoras," by Iamblichus
   (Thomas Taylor's Translation) 285
On "Letters from a Chinese Official" 286
On Colonel Charles A. Lindbergh 286
To A Conscientious Mother 288
On Friendship 289
On Inner Peace 290

Light from the Mountain-tops 290
"The Caravan Moves On" 291
On Self-Confidence and Courage 292
On the Universal Brotherhood and Theosophical
    Society 294
On the Sacred Obligations of a Theosophist ... 295
On the Value of Time and Theosophical Responsibilities 304
A Heart-Message to the Little Folk all over
    the World 306

PREFACE

I HAVE just finished reading the proofs of Katherine Tingley's latest book, THE VOICE OF THE SOUL, and even more than all the others of the present Theosophical Teacher's works, does this book impress me with its deep and tender pathos and its striking imagery of thought.

Good books are so rare; helpful ones rarer still; rarest of all, perhaps, are books like this one in which a truly sublime teaching is given without any pretense whatsoever towards a usage of those artificial and meretricious literary formulae which offend more often than they please.

Great thoughts need no artificial ornamentation. Jewels of the soul have their own inner fire, and sparkle with that divine light which springs from the inner fount of man's spiritual being; and I think that this characteristic of unspoiled beauty is the noblest literary form, and I recognise that this, Katherine Tingley's new book, has it.

We have here a literary work which requires no labored explanation: because its appeal, coming directly from the spirit-soul of the author, travels inwards directly to the spiritual soul of the reader; and there is instant cognition that what the writer says is truth.

The keynote of THE VOICE OF THE SOUL is compassionate wisdom, cleanly expressed. Such was the form which the Messages of all the world's Teachers took, without a single exception known to me; and for this reason have those Messages endured through time, and have become the cherished companions of thoughtful minds. At the fireside, by the bedside, in the study, one reads those works, and receives from them the peace and quiet of mind and the elevation of soul which men and women are so anhungered for.

The world is restless because it feels this hunger of the soul; the hurly-burly of the frenzied thoroughfares of our cities kills all inspiration, and replaces it with the fevered quest for more and more, ay, ever more, satisfying of the appetite for sensational diversions of many different kinds. Indeed, it is a marvel how men and women today can keep for themselves steady brains and clean minds and sweet unpolluted thoughts!

For these reasons is it such a relief to turn to a book like this, and like Katherine Tingley's other noble works, and find in their teachings such sweet repose, and the soothing and tranquillizing influence which emanates from a true Teacher's heart.

Such teachings are the highest mysticism, for the reasons that I have above said, and are expressed in the best mystical form, because free from adventitious and distracting ornaments, so-called, which but embarrass, indeed cripple, the wings of one's own soul in its search for truth and light.

Katherine Tingley's books make me think of beautiful flowers. They are silent, yet they speak in the Silence with tones of power.

Look, when next you cross a flowered

field, at the beautiful blooms springing in profusion under your footsteps; or pass a cultivated garden, pluck therefrom one of the blooms, gaze deep into the heart of it, and you will see a revelation that is priceless — if you have but the eyes to see! Yet it is there for all who will see it; and such is this book, THE VOICE OF THE SOUL, in particular. It is a noble Flower of Thought.

As the eye passes over the pages, the mind drinks in, as it were, the liquid fragrance of the spirit, and one's whole nature is braced upwards and invigorated by the feeling that one is touching, indeed has passed, the frontiers which separate the things of the spirit from those of the flesh.

There is no prating in these books, no mere preaching of fine themes, in which there is no appeal to live the lessons taught. On the contrary, there is intellectual and spiritual stimulation, and moral help. Best of all, perhaps, the perspicacious student finds in them refreshing rest and peace and inspiration.

The entire tenor of Katherine Tingley's

books, and of this one in particular, I think, is the iteration in precept and in lesson, and its reiteration of these, that all the secrets of life are in man's spiritual heart: for there is the fountain of virtue; there is the source of inspiration; there lie greatness and goodness: and what is all this but the teaching of the sages of all the ages?

On page 70, the Theosophical Teacher has the following paragraph:

"Continuous and confident virtue comes from the knowledge of one's soul-life. It is the expression of the strength of the inner man — that part of one which does noble things, aspires to do them, and is ever restless until one has done them."

This is the keynote of the present book, it seems to me; at least I so construe it, for that is the appeal it makes to me personally.

On pages 63 and 64 of the proofs which are before me, I find the following very noble thoughts:

"My endeavor is to give you a conception

of the importance of a man's life when he has found that he has an inner nature, and that it is wholly dependable; that he has within himself those rare and wonderful resources for self-restoration, so to speak. In the inner chambers of our natures there are wonderful mysteries. If we could fathom these, we should have a true companionship with the inner Self, and that inner Self is of abiding, eternal character.

"Do not try to fashion yourselves like others. Dare to think sufficiently long and sufficiently deeply to receive a revelation from within. Make clean self-analysis a regular habit. Take ten minutes with yourself every day, and absolutely surrender your mental self to your Higher Self. Then you will open for yourself a book of revelations."

Anyone who has any knowledge whatsoever of ancient literatures will recognise in the foregoing extracts from THE VOICE OF THE SOUL, the very core of the meaning of the injunction given by golden Apollo through his oracle at Delphi, and which was so famous in the ancient world: MAN, KNOW THYSELF! Likewise does the sacred literature of ancient Hindûsthân teach the same secret of being, pre-eminently in those noble works the Upanishads, and there also the emphasis was laid still more strongly upon the fact of the deathless Self, a ray of the Universal Self of the universe.

When a man knows himself he knows the inmost secrets of being, for he has within himself, nay, is himself in his inmost essence, the Universal Self, as I have just said, and therefore can draw upon his inner nature from inexhaustible streams of wisdom and knowledge.

There are no riddles which the aspiring spirit of man may not solve. There are no secrets of Nature or of man's self which a courageous research into the recesses and arcana of his own inner fora will not give him. How extraordinary is it not then that men should turn away from that fountain of all truth, and seek truth in sources outside of it!

The inmost of us is at all times a Poet, a Sage, a Philosopher, a Genius, a Revealer, a Savior, because ever drawing upon those Pierian Springs which arise from the Fountain of Universal Being.

Put in philosophical language and philosophical terminology, this expresses the teaching of this book, THE VOICE OF THE SOUL. I know it because I have found it there. These books by Katherine Tingley are my constant companions, and every time that I take one of them up, it seems to me that I pass a step farther forward into those wondrous realms of the frontierless consciousness of the spirit, of which I have just spoken.

I suppose that no thinking human can find anything to object to in the strangely appealing manner in which Katherine Tingley has written in this book, and indeed in her other books; I doubt if the veriest bigot, whose atrabilious temperament, through miseducation, views things alway awry, could see in this noble work aught that could be successfully criticized, or reasonably objected to, from the standpoint of wisdom or truth.

How different is the series of books, which Katherine Tingley has given to the world, from the ordinary religious or philosophical writings of the day, in which the authors seem bent upon producing material for controversy, or the airing of personal views rather than the delivery of sheer truth.

Student: man, woman, or child; Reader: religious or philosophic or scientific: drink freely of these Pierian Springs!

I have said enough: here is the book itself.

G. VON PURUCKER

International Theosophical Headquarters,
Point Loma, California,
April, 1928.

SECTION I

The Voice of the Soul

"The human heart has not yet fully uttered itself."— H. P. BLAVATSKY

THE VOICE OF THE SOUL

IF the soul of man could be recognised in the truest and fullest sense, there would be the revelation of a new life, new trust, new understandings; and then in sequence would follow a change in the lives of all humanity for the better.

The Soul is the Real Man

How few there are who approach the question of man's soul and grasp it with the understanding that would naturally be theirs if they had the slightest idea of the existence of the soul!

The real message of the soul, and its divine mission, are not sufficiently understood to enable man to know himself; for as soon as the mind is enlightened by soul-forces that are appealed to through the mentality, there comes the revelation that I teach, and the answers to our questionings which we are craving to hear.

How little is said or taught about the soul-life, and its complete identification with the human being! To most men the soul is something apart from themselves, that is only to be talked of and trusted in on special occasions; there is no real companionship, no intimate affiliation, between men's minds and souls in their every-day existence. Now, according to the teachings of Theosophy, there is in every man a divine power, and when that divinity, which is his real Self, is acknowledged and understood by the mind, it takes a very active part in man's life; indeed, it should fill at the very least one-half of his thought-life.

When we have this full view of the identity of man with the soul clearly in mind, then we move outside the ordinary way of thinking and find ourselves on a new path, daring to think towards the unknowable, the seeming impossible. In doing this, we bring into action the soul.

According to my philosophy, every normal child when it is born is enveloped and covered and protected so to speak, with soul-forces, though invisible. We must not think of the soul as something apart from ourselves, as something that occupies a special compartment in our brains or in our thoughts; for every time a child is born, through the operation of those sacred and wonderful laws of Nature which men do not yet understand, it has the spiritual backing, the spiritual support, the divine enfoldment, of the soul; and if the child is rightly understood, this spiritual part will be at least as fully recognised as the material part.

How many children, alas, go wrong! How many dear parents wear their lives out trying to bring their children up rightly! When I think of the failures along this line, it looks to me as though the ignorance, the stupidity, the selfishness, and the egoism of the age had turned the children directly away from these soul-forces and launched them out into the world without their support. We cannot see these refined and wonderful forces of Nature; we cannot easily describe them nor can we fully measure them. It is not for us to understand them fully, yet we all catch glimpses of them.

If we would spend one-half as much time in thinking of our future from the standpoint of ourselves as souls, essentially divine, as we do in thinking of our material wants and needs, we should be so free from many of the trials and difficulties that we have to contend with that we should think we already had found the Kingdom of Heaven on earth.

A child should be nourished with spiritual food and care, as much as with material food and care.

Every true mother has at least some understanding of the spiritual laws of her own being from the beginning of the gestation of the child. With her love and care she carries the child, envelops it, holds it, and serves it with what knowledge she has; and when the child is born, in her innermost thoughts she knows that there are two sides to the little one entrusted to her care: on the one hand there is the immortal, the divine, the eternal and real essence of the child's character brought over from previous lives; and on the other hand there is the material body, itself produced in a mysterious, almost magical way, from a tiny seed.

Some day our courageous scientists are going to find out and reveal to the whole world the truth of what I am now saying. It would take a great deal of courage for one of them to step out at present and talk as I am talking. He probably could not do it and hold his position before the world. But it will not be more than twenty-five or fifty years before some of these wonderful secrets of human nature which have thus far been ignored will be understood and generally accepted.

I hold that the soul of man is seeking to utter itself from the time of its physical incarnation. It knows its birthrights; it knows more than is apparent. But it is thrust into the world under very adverse circumstances; and the child is fed, cared for, loved, and nurtured as a physical being and as little more, with the vague possibility of having a future life somewhere or somehow.

But Theosophy teaches us that we are sacredly and divinely made and built for this life; and only by understanding the lives of our children, approaching and reaching them from the standpoint of spiritual knowledge, can the soul speak.

Now some people may say: "All this is too abstruse, it is too far away, and we have no way of proving it." Well, there are thousands of things in the lives of men and women that cannot be proved; they do not even understand themselves, and are mysteries to themselves. When a child is born, can the father and mother explain the profound mysteries of how that soul came into physical incarnation — of the processes that took place when from a seed the child stepped out into our universe, radiant in its spiritual potentialities, although not visible to the human eye — and became a part of the human family? If we know so little about the creation of physical life, how can we expect parents to have the information needed for them to do full justice to their child in the spiritual sense?

Our great scientific thinkers accomplish

wonders in very many ways; but unless they dare to face the unknown, unless they have imagination that stretches out beyond time and space almost, unless they recognise the higher imagination as a spiritual and divine attribute of the soul instead of a faculty useful only for the play of fancy, to entertain or to give pleasure, they will never hear the Voice of the Soul. *Imagination a Divine Attribute of the Soul*

Let us reach basic truths. We must study causes. We do not study them enough. The usual way is to study effects — especially with the unfortunate. We put them in jail, keep them locked up there, and then, supposing ourselves to be the great authorities on earth, we assume that we have a legal right to destroy their bodies sometimes and to violate their souls nearly always. Yes, the Twentieth Century still allows such things!

Humanity is drifting, drifting, drifting! Something must happen to bring about a change in the chaotic life that we are leading. Twenty years ago we would have been terrified to read once a year of the shocking, outrageous crimes that now we hear of almost daily!

We may not see it ourselves, but the fact is that we men and women of the great human family are at present retrograding, we are going down-hill, we are neglecting our most sacred duties, we are losing our way: we are ignoring the soul, we are turning our backs to the light, we are afraid to step out and venture in thought, in action, in will-power and determination, into the unknown, and with imagination to visualize the dignity of the soul of man.

Let us seek to awaken in our growing children a consciousness of the nearness of this affectionate, indescribable something which I have called the Soul. Teach them that they are not thrown out into this world alone, that they are not ignored, but that they are enveloped in the soul-life and possess the inner wisdom with which they were born. Then with the environment that our children can have through the intelligence of the parents, and with the noble examples that should be set by every man and woman on the face of the earth, the voice of the soul would be heard and recognised.

We should not have to address prayers to a personal God, or to make any of those woeful sacrifices that so many people think they must make in order to 'square up their accounts with the Creator.' What is necessary is that we should all challenge ourselves with the questions: "Who am I? Why am I here?"

The closer we come to the beauties and realities of Nature, the more quickly shall we begin to feel the power of the soul-life. But alas! there are so many distractions and allurements in the world. Then, too, there is the bread-and-butter question that has to be solved. There are poverty and suffering and vice and crime that must be faced; and these things are not lessening, they are increasing.

We must dare to do something more than we ever did before, not dare to do anything dishonorable or out of place, but we must dare to step up higher, to climb. We must dare to do it alone without public heralding or recognition, but just within the silence of our own soul, of our own conscience. This superb opportunity is right at hand for all.

With all the scientific discoveries and ideas that are being constantly brought out concerning children and human nature generally and a thousand other subjects, it is only a very, very few scientists who have sufficient imagination or daring to attempt to penetrate into the realm of the seemingly impossible, and to bring back with them for the benefit of humanity something really worth while. So, in spite of the great mass of scientific facts which have been accumulated, we go on day after day drifting and drifting, until we have drifted beyond all likelihood of recovering our anchorage in this lifetime. Then, alas! what regrets and tears and despair!

There comes the question: "Why has not somebody done something?" It is because nearly everybody is waiting for everybody else! In spiritual efforts we do not need to wait for unity. Let every man and every woman act for himself or herself according to the individual evolution and enlightenment. One must have the disposition and the daring to act alone, indifferent to results so far as they affect himself or herself, so long as the motive is pure.

When we reach this state of mind, we shall see more smiles on the faces of the mothers and fathers, less anxiety on their features. We shall see new cheer in the world, new evidences of purity in the lives of men and women, and consequently more purity and more joy in the children of the masses. This is the way to reach our children and to enable them to hear the Voice of the Soul — of that divine part of us that is our real Self. We could not exist without it.

But, on the other hand, there is the picture before me of how this innate divinity is ignored, how it is thrown aside, and how it takes nearly a lifetime for people, even of the highest intelligence striving to do their best in order to gain knowledge, to reach the first fundamental idea of their own soul-life. It is true that we have the opportunities for wonderful scholastic education; our country as a whole has plenty of wealth, great territory, and an over-abundance of public laudation of our outer material progress and prosperity. But the inner life — that silent power that speaks to us as the Voice of the Soul — is very largely ignored.

No one of us can find the meaning of real affection, of spiritual love, unless we find it alone. I am referring to that deeper love, that spiritual companionship of the soul which is ours at our best and highest moments. Mothers sometimes have it in their experience of motherhood. It speaks to them without words. The Voice of the Soul whispers to them in the silences. The brain-mind does not fully comprehend it, and consequently the pleadings of the Voice of the Soul are not always heeded.

To me one of the most beautiful experiences in life is to retire into the inner sanctuary of one's own being, away from all the rush and so-called allurements of the outer life, and in the silence to listen to the Voice of the Soul, to hear its pleadings, to know its power, to clasp hands with the spiritual soul, the Higher Self, so to speak, to work with it and walk with it and live with it. A man must do this before he can be absolutely sure of anything.

Theosophy the Key

Hence it is that I dare to say that Theosophy is filled with glowing fires of helpfulness that cannot be found anywhere else in fullness. There is no question that there are many beautiful ideas in all religions, and among their adherents are very splendid people who make most praiseworthy efforts. But they have not the key that would give them the wider knowledge and the deeper wisdom; and without this key they can go only so far and no farther.

Consequently, if one studies the inner condition of some of our great religious organizations, one will find in them a deterioration; they are falling down. Indeed, there are numbers of strong men and women within their ranks who dare to come out openly and admit as much. The majority have been so carried away with the letter of their religious teachings that they have lost sight of the inner spirit; they have been living so much in the forms and the formalities of their religion and away from the truth of the inner life, that decay is in the air.

It would, of course, be not only unjust but absurd to say that there are not good and noble principles in the heart of every man and woman and at the core of every sincere religious system. But we want the better thing; we want the complete thing; we want the full knowledge that belongs to us in this life.

If I go to school, I am entitled to a full educational equipment, provided I reach out for it. But I must get it by application and conscientious work. So it is with the wider schooling of each earth-life. I must get it by devotion, by understanding the fundamental principles and ideas upon which I hope to live, and by a harmonious relationship with my fellow-men and my environment. Then I may know something about the Voice of the Soul.

I am very much interested in the minds of men and women and in their serious thoughts. One finds, of course, very beautiful ideas in the literatures of the world. But I have made a life-long study of criminology, not for my amusement, but for the knowledge that I might gain in order to help those whom I worked for: I was very actively engaged in work among prisoners and unfortunates even before I was identified with the Theosophical Society.

I am always looking for evidences in my reading of something said or done that shows intelligent human understanding of and sympathy for the most degraded, the most forgotten, the most ignored,— and according to the old dogmatic religious idea the most damned. But I am sorry to say that I do not find much of such understanding and sympathy. On the other hand, everywhere there is severe criticism, cries for harsher punishment.

Recently I was reading in a newspaper that some of the authorities representing the State of California, I believe, in the prosecution of young Hickman, called upon him in his cell — this unfortunate, pitiful specimen of a promising youth gone wrong — in order to find out from him his choice(!) as to how they should dispose of his body after he shall have been hanged — whether it should go to his mother or to some medical institution for an autopsy!

Now, when our public conscience has become as callous as that, it is time that we went to school; it is time that we acquired some of the spiritual knowledge that I speak of; it is time that we hearkened to the Voice of the Soul so that we might find the way to Light. Because of the lack of this knowledge and of the part that the soul takes in the growth and evolution of humanity, our civilization today is all awry.

I was talking with a lady a few days ago and she asked me: "How can the soul be redeemed?" I told her that I had never given any thought to such a question, for the reason that the spiritual soul itself is so potent that it will redeem mankind if people will only hearken to its voice.

Redemption and the Voice of the Soul

We do not have to fashion any special form or way of bringing people to redemption. Just give them the opportunity to be themselves — their real selves, their higher selves. Do not try to dictate to them; do not drive them; but challenge them! Cowards are they who do not make the effort to liberate their souls from the bondage in which selfishness and weakness hold them!

It is the inner laws that are the realities; and because humanity does not know about them nor understand them, it has been fighting the realities!

Enlarge your vision! Dare to climb! Dare to go forward! Dare to think for yourselves and to look ahead! Question! Put yourselves in order! When you do this, revelations will come to you — not in any magical way with visions or messages from 'on high,' nor anything of that sort. But let me illustrate by the growth of children. If one sees them from day to day one is hardly aware that they are growing; yet to those who see them only at long intervals their growth is very evident.

The fact is that the divine forces and processes which bring a child from a seed — so small that a hundred of them can be placed on a one-inch strand of a spider's web — into babyhood, and from babyhood through childhood to manhood or womanhood: these processes, so delicate, so infinitely and spiritually refined, are taken care of by the laws of life, which are only partially understood even by our most learned scientists. But I cannot conceive how they are to be fully understood without studying Theosophy. Still less can the process of man's spiritual growth and unfoldment be understood without some knowledge of the Ancient Wisdom, Theosophy.

There is no attempt on the part of a true Theosophist to 'convert' anyone. We have no method of 'conversion.' We certainly never use any influence to persuade anyone to join our Society.

And most assuredly we never menace

people with the threat that their souls will be lost if they do not accept our teachings. We do nothing of that sort. We simply tell people: "Here are our books. From them you can gain much knowledge." But the real inner knowledge comes from the courageous stepping out of ordinary ruts into the great broad blue of life, and from looking at Nature as it is — courageously.

Study the trees and the flowers, and the ocean, and the wonders of the life around you. Notice the growth of a tree. During the spring-time it will put forth green leaves, then its exquisite blossoms, and in the summer-time it will bear its fruit. After a while it is bereft of leaves, blossoms, and fruit — of everything that was beautiful and attractive. It appears dead. But the inner life is continuing all through the season of quiet and rest. The processes of inner growth are taking place. How wonderful in the spring-time, when the tree bursts forth into beautiful foliage again! Who can question that preparation was going on all during the sleeping-season?

So it is with the flowers that cover our fields and fill our homes and beautify everything. In them we can see the wonderful working of the Divine Law. We must feel it and know it and find our lessons in it, not simply admire the outward beauty.

But you cannot feel it by study alone. You can get a touch of it only by daring to step forth and to think thoughts quite apart, if necessary, from anybody else's. Then you will be really climbing in the spiritual sense.

Seek the companionship of the Silence, for the Silence is the most precious companion in the world.

Some day expectant mothers will go forth into their retreats, as they used to do in ancient times, living the most abstemious and beautiful life, in touch with Nature; not tied down with family difficulties and cares and cross-purposes and poverty, and so forth, but filling their souls with the music and the joy of Nature — calling out the Voice of the Soul. When that time arrives, then we may honestly talk of a new and far better generation.

That will be the answer to the woman who asked what were the processes by which we could redeem the soul. It is the soul that will redeem humanity. There are as many processes as there are human beings — each must work out his own salvation according to his environment and his enlightenment.

In the deepest spiritual sense we are all united, though not on the outward plane. But because we have differed so much and so long, and have moved so far away from the great principles of life, we have lost the secret of living together in outer harmony. Yet in the inner life we are still working together in unity, in harmony with the divine laws, understanding them and obeying them in the dignity of true manhood and womanhood.

Let us teach our children the better way! No more jails! No more prisons! No more reformatories! But let the children hear every day in their own home the Voice of the Soul!

Those adults who are single and have no homes, can make a home for themselves in their own hearts, in their memories; and the divine power of the soul can enlighten them and impress the mind with better things.

Two things cannot occupy the same place at the same time; and if the mind is filled with high incentives, beautiful principles, royal, splendid and uplifting efforts, the Voice of the Soul speaks, and the evil and weaknesses born of the undeveloped and selfish side of our human nature cannot come in; so they will die out. Then we shall not have to punish or hang our fellow-men or do anything of that sort.

I am very sure that if we could scour the country today, we should find more culprits and criminals still free and unrecognised than behind the bars. It is the vices and insincerities of these stealthy 'respectable' criminals that are the deathly destroyers of our homes and of our civilization.

It is distressing to me at times to think of our children growing up in the public schools. Certainly the teachers there are doing their very best — indeed, they do wonders, I think, when one considers the gap there is between the school and the home, and the little support and co-operation that the teachers frequently receive from over-indulgent or ignorant parents.

The Training of Children

But even where there is co-operation by the parents, the teacher's influence and ability to help the children individually is very limited; first, because of the large number that each teacher must look after, and secondly, because the teacher cannot be responsible for what goes on outside of school-hours.

Children, you know, are very susceptible to all kinds of influences — good and bad, helpful and undesirable, whatever happens to come their way. A hint for parents and teachers: whenever you see children forming into little coteries or cliques, the members of which try to be together whenever they can, if you understand human nature as well as I do from my long experience in supervising the education of children, you will be on the lookout. Children in such coteries are nearly always drifting in the wrong direction.

It is a dangerous symptom when either

children or adults become dependent upon any particular acquaintance for companionship. Beware! Friendship must be based upon something deeper and nobler than special attachments and mutual admiration and flattery, which generally lead to unwholesome personal relations.

It is difficult to recognise the soul, to hear the voice of the divine in man, until you have found Theosophy. This I declare.

The Voice of the Soul is the Voice of the Universe, in all its wonderful manifestations. How remarkably and clearly and divinely it speaks to us through all the days and nights of our lives! And yet, to a very large degree, we heed it not. The Voice of the Soul is also the divine quality in every human heart; and it is this aspect of my subject that I refer to more especially.

I have often referred to the birth or the coming into incarnation of little children. The laws of Nature, or 'the laws of God'— in either case the Divine Laws — have prepared everything for the incoming of souls;

but is it not possible that we humans with our limited knowledge of divine things, and our still more limited practice of them, have failed to accentuate or to emphasize the divine side of life for the little children?

I suppose that every mother who has any spiritual aspirations at all, knows intuitively that her little one is a ray of the Divine in essence, that it is a spiritual soul. But it must be admitted that far more time and care are given to the child's material needs than are devoted to its spiritual unfoldment; and it cannot be denied that many, many parents are pitifully unprepared for the reception of the souls that come into their homes. Everywhere there is ignorance or inadequate knowledge. The result is that from the beginning of its earth-life the child is bereft of one-half of its rightful heritage.

A child will develop as naturally in harmony with the divine laws as with man-made laws, customs, and practices, many of which are far-fetched and quite unessential. If the soul-qualities of man were undisturbed from the very beginning of childhood, we would have a higher and a better expression of babyhood, of boyhood and girlhood, and inevitably of manhood and womanhood.

Think of the wrecks along the way — of the many boys now behind the bars who were once mothers' darlings. Most of these may have been fairly well taken care of in the physical sense. But morally they are lacking. This does not necessarily mean that the parents neglected doing anything that they knew they should do; but not having been educated themselves to understand the importance of depending on the moral and spiritual laws, they cannot impart what they themselves have not in their own makeup. This may possibly explain in a satisfactory way why humanity is all awry.

There are thousands going or striving to go the right way; but, alas! there are also thousands going the other way. There is little harmony in the great human family. One may find harmony in the flowers, in the trees, and in the silence of Nature, and in the stars above us; but in human life it is nowhere to be found. People may have their *Self-aspirations*, their prayers, their desires; they *Directed* may also have a splendid scholastic educa-*Evolution* tion; they may even be ranked as geniuses; but the one great thing that humanity is hungering for, asking for, pleading for, and yearning for, is not to be found in the deepest sense.

If I had my life to live over again, and could be free from some of the responsibilities that are mine now, my whole aim in my teaching, my writing, my lecturing, and in the example of my life, would be to lead people on to the path of self-directed evolution, in order that we humans might bring into every act of our daily lives the high, noble, and splendid things that are right at hand, and can be taken in at any moment.

There is no question that thousands are striving and have the disposition to make worthy efforts; but they are all fettered by the lack of knowledge. They have not the one great key that H. P. Blavatsky brought to the modern world. This key is Theosophy, the Ancient Wisdom-Religion. It lifts the veil; it opens the way; it answers your questions; it dispels your doubts and your fears. The keys to real knowledge, which Theosophy offers, are so simple that any normal child of intelligence can understand them.

Beware of Counterfeit Theosophy

Now, while the Universal Brotherhood and Theosophical Society, which I have the honor of directing, is the original Theosophical Society founded by that glorious and splendid woman, H. P. Blavatsky, in New York in 1875, still we cannot hold any monopoly of the name 'Theosophy.' Though, as already stated, her message, Theosophy, was really the Wisdom-Religion of Antiquity, it was new to the modern world. Hence it was sometimes seized upon by fanatics of different kinds, who chose to use it for self-aggrandisement — in order to attract personal devotees, and in some instances in order to make money.

So, pitiful to relate, pseudo-Theosophy has been taught in nearly every large city throughout the world in the most absurd, outrageous, and distressing manner, far removed from the original teachings of pure Theosophy. Thus many serious-minded truth-seekers have actually been turned away from the light of genuine Theosophy, because they have come into touch with these pseudo-theosophists, who through their sensational advertising have used the name in spreading their own wild teachings, which generally appeal to wonder-seekers alone.

One of the latest of such efforts has been to impress people all over the world with the fantastic idea that quite an ordinary Hindû lad is "a coming Christ"—"a new Messiah"! This attempt, however, was rather too much of a strain on people's credulity, and the plans failed in the truest sense. Nevertheless there are still many people who have been caught up in this vortex of misunderstanding everything that pertains to man's higher life — to the beauty of life, the harmony of life, and the justice of life.

For this reason, perhaps, the earnest members of the Universal Brotherhood and

Theosophical Society work so hard to present
Man Reli- to the public the real teachings of Theoso-
gious by phy; likewise we aim to practise extreme
Nature patience and genuine love for humanity.

Think of the isms, the fads, the fantastic notions, and the madnesses that have been presented to the world in the name of Religion! But this last effort that I have referred to as being made in the name of Theosophy is about the worst. No wonder that these isms make people lose faith in religion, in their consciences, and in their duty! No wonder that they lose faith in their God! No wonder that they ignore the lofty teaching of man's essential divinity, and are misled!

Yet according to the teachings of Theosophy, we are religious beings by nature, the soul-life being an essential part of ourselves — the real, eternal man. The rest of man dies when the body dies, including the brain-mind upon which we all depend so much,— and upon which we should indeed depend to a large degree. All the mental faculties, including personal memory, die when the physical man dies. But the real man, the spiritual man, lives on forever.

Man's spiritual nature is difficult to understand for most people, because it is supposed to be difficult to prove. But there are thousands of things in the world today that are true and we have to accept them, even though we cannot prove them. Man's spiritual nature is so refined and so etherealized in a sense, that it is difficult to prove it formally. Nevertheless it is visible to the inner eye.

But you must have the vision to see it; you must have the ears to hear its message: and you must know what you are seeking. You must reach out for it, and your life must be in harmony with your aspirations; you must not play angel today and demon tomorrow; you must not do good today and tomorrow deceive yourselves and your friends. You must be true to the inner quality of your own nature — the divine spark, the ray of the Universal Life. Be true to that, and all other good things will come to you.

The great human race must see more than it now sees, must hear more than it now hears, must know more than it now knows. But the difficulty is that for thousands of years we have been held back by false teachings which have given a backward turn to human nature. If our blood could be analysed by a spiritual chemist, we should find that the very atoms of our body are tinctured with the errors that we have been taught all down the ages. The result is that when our hearts might urge us to leap forward in search of spiritual truth, or when we might feel a touch of divine inspiration for the moment, there comes the contrary impulse of the doubting nature that shuts out the light.

There is a thousand times more to be discovered in human life than we know already. There is enough light in this great universe of ours to bring to the whole human race a song of eternal peace, of a quality that would keep humanity always together.

In the truest sense we are all members

of one great Universal Brotherhood, we are all of 'God's great family.' But in the outward sense we are frightfully divided.

The Optimism of Theosophy

The power of Theosophy and its divine touch are to be found in the help that there is in it for men and women, in the guidance that it provides, and in the enlightenment that it gives.

In looking into the teachings of Theosophy, one who is seeking for more knowledge soon reaches the conviction that he is treading the right road; he feels that there is something ahead; he hears the Voice of the Soul. But there must be continuity of effort.

Think for a moment of the creations of our men of genius. If they had stopped and turned back in doubt at the time when the divine impulse touched them, we should have no grand music, no beautiful paintings, no inspired art, no marvelous inventions. These splendid, uplifting, creative forces originally come from man's divine nature.

If we all lived in the consciousness and

the conviction of our own great possibilities, we should realize that we are souls, and that we too have divine privileges far beyond anything that we know of or even think of. Yet we throw these aside, because they are not acceptable to our limited, personal selves. They do not fit in with our preconceived ideas.

So we forget that we are a part of the divine Scheme of Life, that the meaning of life is sacred and holy; and we allow ourselves to drift back into the vortex of misunderstanding, misconception, doubt, unhappiness, and despair.

Theosophy, on the other hand, is optimistic. The moment when its teachings touch the heart of a man or a woman, there is a lifting of the spirit; there is a new fire burning within; there are new pulsations in the heart; there is a new brightness in the eyes; there is a new joy for that soul. It may not perhaps be spoken of or described, but something has come into that life. That soul steps out on the path of self-directed evolution — evolution directed by his own higher nature; and he moves along that road with a conviction that the ultimate relative perfection of man is assured. *Man's Essential Divinity*

A soul that starts on the path that I have spoken of, finds the companionship of his own essential divinity. He is conscious of an increasing knowledge, so delicate, so refined, so subtil, and so far away from the senses, that no language can express it. It is something akin to that mystical quality that touches the human heart when the word 'love' is devoutly uttered — a touch of the divine.

Along this path of self-directed evolution one meets of course many crossways. Disappointments visit him. But think what an appeal there is to the brave man to continue the journey! He is marching on in response to the challenge of his own soul, of the divine quality within himself.

As he moves forward, he will begin to find the reality of things which he had formerly ignored. Sacred blessings will come to him without money and without price. He will find the beginning of great joy, the beginning of a new life, the beginning of sublime efforts, and a quality of courage that will enable him to proclaim from the housetops and the mountain-tops, anywhere and everywhere, that man is essentially divine: and that is the voice and the music of the soul, seeking expression in the hearts of men.

Humanity is hungry for its spiritual food, for that quality of soul-nourishment that should have been given in childhood, but is given only occasionally when the mother is at the height of her aspirations for her child, when she is thinking in the silence and praying to her God for something better. Then she hears the Voice of the Soul. But the pity is that she cannot hear it continuously — from lack of unison between the inner and the outer life.

There is little co-operation but much fearful division in the minds of men and women, and in the forms and customs of society. These things are the enemies of our progress as long as we allow them to be.

The Voice of the Soul is seeking expression in the outer world, in order to bring to the recognition of men the real spirit of brotherhood, that spiritual unity that belongs to us, that inner fire which marks us as religious in essence, religious by birth, religious by heredity, religious because it is instinctively felt that justice and truth will ultimately manifest themselves.

By listening to the Voice of the Soul one becomes not only a good man, but a noble man, a holy man, and a blessing to all the world.

I lived during my childhood in Massachusetts. My home-life in the summer-time was in the woodlands on the banks of the beautiful Merrimac, immortalized by Whittier. Much of my young life was spent in the company of a very great man, and yet a very simple man, quite unrecognised by the world for his remarkable virtues. He was my grandfather, who, under peculiar circumstances, had asked for and had finally obtained the right personally to control my education.

I have no recollection of anything irksome or hard that I had to learn from him. I always felt that my real teacher, if it can be called a teacher, was within myself. Even as a child I used to talk in this way, which led my father to fear that by the time I was twenty-one years of age I would be somewhat demented, or something of that sort! Nevertheless, the conviction that my real teacher was within me, was very strong.

When I was four or five years old, I used to disturb my people by telling them that I heard the trees sing, and many things along that line, which seemed very uncanny to people of those days in New England, where the power of dogmatism and convention was very strong. So all through my childhood I led quite an isolated life, except for the inspiring companionship of my grandfather.

It was not the intention of my father or mother that I should mark my life with any eccentricities or peculiarities. So the path that I should follow was laid out with conventional precision. My father secured the services of the best teachers and musicians, but I never could learn from them. I do not mean by this that I was anything remarkable at all; on the contrary, I was considered a sort of freak.

But sometimes I improvised, and at other times I had very clear mind-pictures of the future: one of which was of the 'White City' that I should some day build in the 'Gold-Land' of the West, where I should gather together children of all nations and teach them how to live rightly.

In communion with my grandfather, there was one thing that impressed me very strongly, small as I was, and I have never forgotten it: the most beautiful memory I have of him is that what he preached he lived.

My father too was a very delightful and splendid man; I loved him dearly. But he was a materialist, and had little in common with my thoughts or my grandfather's.

To a very large degree, my grandfather

and I understood each other, and our understanding was expressed more in the silence than in words. Whenever I think of him, I am always impressed with the fact that the soul of that man was so much alive that he was ever conscious of its presence and guidance.

When I grew older I said to him: "Is it because I love you so, or am I right in feeling that when you speak, something besides that great intellect of yours is speaking — something different from what I hear and see?"

In a very simple way he answered: "It is the Voice of the Soul that you hear. The soul could speak in all men did they but keep the conscience clear, trust in the Divine Law, and live for a high purpose."

"What is that purpose?" I asked.

"There are a great many high purposes," he answered; "but the one purpose above all others, is so to live as to be a benefit to humanity."

He was my first ideal of a great character.

He was the first outward proof that I had that man in his innermost nature is divine.

I remember when I was a little girl, I worked very hard to avoid going to an extremely orthodox church. On account of this I was considered very eccentric, and so I was let alone, and that was the happiest time of my life.

When others went to church, I would skip out into the woods with my dog. It was there that I learned some of the great secrets of life.

I think that every lesson that I received came first through the woodlands, from the birds and the flowers, or from thoughts stimulated by being there. It was there that I found myself; it was there that I found the little spiritual strength that I had. It was there that I had the vision in a sense that real life was wonderful and beautiful, but that humanity as a whole was living in the valley of the shadows, because as a people we had not reached up higher, we had not trusted ourselves, because we had been hemmed in by the false teachings of the past.

Many things that I read in the Bible I found very interesting, but there were other parts that I could not accept at all. I never had accepted the idea that we were born in sin, nor from that time until now have I ever believed in a personal God. Nevertheless, my thoughts dwelt very much upon the spiritual side of life.

We have quite enough of the outer side of life all the time; in fact, we are oppressed with it, we are actually persecuted by it. But when we seek to find the soul of things, we must search for something within ourselves, so that we may gain confidence in ourselves. When we have this, and carry with us daily and hourly the beautiful, uplifting, and enlightening thoughts that come from such trust and such confidence, Theosophy teaches that everything else is cared for.

There is nothing that is right but what is permissible.

In the deeper sense there is no such thing

as chance in life; but everything is a part of the universal laws. As far as we choose to work with them, to clasp hands with them, or embrace them, so to speak, though we see them not, we feel them in our innermost natures, in our hearts, and their light shines through our eyes. Thus we work in harmony with the divine qualities within ourselves, and we make the great wheel of human evolution move more rapidly forward towards the goal of ultimate perfection.

We Theosophists hold that man is something more than most of us ever dream of being, and that the divine qualities of man are seeking to express themselves in every hour that we live, almost in every breath that we take. But the larger number of people have depended so long on the mentality alone that spiritual knowledge has been to a large degree ignored.

The mind of man is indeed a wonderful power. When rightly used it can be a guide and a help; but it is not the highest part of man's nature. When this higher part impresses the mentality with those inspirations that distinguish real men and women from merely human beings, it brings joy into life to replace the travesty on real life that we see all about us.

Then one can speak of the soul of man. Then one can know how beautiful, how superb, how grand, the spiritual things in life really are. Then one realizes that just as today is an experience, and tomorrow another experience, so is a lifetime just one experience in the progress of the soul of man towards perfection. It is not the only one; there are more and more, and still more.

Thus the soul advances, becomes strong, grows powerful, and at last has the foresight to direct its own destiny.

If a man will set his feet firmly on the path of self-directed evolution, believing in the eternal verities that make life joy, that make life peace, that make life powerful and just, then he will begin to hear the Voice of the Soul.

Years ago I once heard Henry Ward

Beecher speak. Some time afterwards he went through a great trial. There was a shadow in his church; there was talk of having him depart because he had been indiscreet. But no one could ever make me believe that there was anything wrong about him, for that man had the light.

Now is the Time

He had a wonderfully impressive mind. He was spiritual in his nature. I have seen his face light up like a god. I do not think, however, that he often gave outward expression to his spiritual inspiration, especially at those times when I have seen him preaching to a fashionable audience, some of whom were half asleep, others busily fanning themselves, and just a few listening. He probably knew that such was not the time to speak.

But there is a time to speak; and I hold that now, while we are suffering still from the effects of that dreadful world-war, and from the indiscretions and the vices and the crimes that afflict our civilization, it is high time that humanity as a whole should awaken.

Dare to believe that tomorrow can be

made better than today! Never be discouraged! Go through life unafraid! In this way you will hear the Voice of the Soul. In this way you will dare and conquer, and move onward toward ever greater achievements.

Even as a child, instead of feeling disdain or dread because I myself had so little real knowledge, I learned to love humanity. Perhaps that is one of the reasons why I am here today, seeking to impress the minds of men with the fact that as yet life is only half lived when you depend upon the mentality alone.

Unless you have a solid foundation on which to build your character, life is a farce or a tragedy; the shadows are heavy, everything is discouraging, pessimism reigns, leading in extreme cases to suicide, and more than all else to the terrible crimes that confront us day by day in ever increasing numbers. A great deal of this I know is the result of the world-war.

Thinking of these things, we have a tremendous duty to perform. We cannot afford to lose one moment in moving away from the light of truth in our own inner natures.

Where did Jesus tell us that the Kingdom of Heaven was to be found? Did he say it was up in the skies? Did he not tell you that the Kingdom of Heaven is within you? This answers nearly all suggestions that might be made in opposition to what I have said about the Voice of the Soul, provided of course you accept Jesus as a Teacher, which I do. I look upon him as a very great Teacher, an inspirer, an initiate, but not as a special son of God.

In the truest sense, Theosophy frees the human mind from thraldom. It enables one to meet the tomorrow without fear, and to look at death as something beautiful. We should not be afraid to think of our dear ones who have passed on. In the real sense they are still living, still loving, still faithful, and still devoted, for real love is eternal. If it is eternal, and if it was yours here, it is yours forever.

Have a little more confidence in your-

The Great Impediments to Spiritual Progress

selves! Do not be so dependent upon your worldly position, upon your intellectual attainments, upon your environment, or upon your personality! Find the Silence within you! Find the peace and quiet of Nature away from the rush and whirl of daily activities! Thus you will be free to know the inner mysteries of life, and you never can do it until you take the first step in that direction.

Meet these teachings half-way, and then apply them to your lives. It is the application that counts. Knowledge is only half-knowledge until it is applied.

One of the greatest impediments to the human mind's grasping its sovereignty or understanding the power of the spiritual life and thus overcoming all difficulties, is the belief in only one earth-life. Here is where the real trouble lies. In all my teaching I am constantly reminding my listeners of the importance of the doctrine of Reincarnation.

I also repeat over and over again that two things cannot occupy the same place at the same time; and that if the mind is oppressed from morning until night not merely with the actual duties of life but with countless non-essentials, it finds itself in the old rut of limiting existence to seventy-seven or a hundred years.

The only reason why people interested in human progress do not rush to Theosophy by the hundreds of thousands, is that they do not want to give up so much — as they imagine; but as a matter of fact all they have to give up is the non-essentials that hold them in slavery to this idea and that, to this opinion and that, to this convention and that, to this dogma and that.

But of course in every age there are a few progressive minds whom we will not attempt to name here, who dare to step outside the beaten path and to take great long breaths of spiritual life. They dare to believe that there is something more in human life than they already know. They dare to acknowledge to themselves that in their silent, their most aspiring, and best moments, there is something beyond this one earth-life.

The soul of man in its dignity, in its sovereignty, in its royalty, gives us the beautiful vista of the continuity of spiritual life.

We are assured that man does not die in the real sense, for the real man, the spiritual entity, is an eternal entity in the great Scheme of Life, and he only seems to die.

But most people in western lands are so absorbed in the delusions of the outer life that they think that they themselves are merely the bodies which they inhabit. They are so psychologized by this idea that when they reach the age of forty-five or fifty they are already planning for the disposal of their worldly belongings and beginning to think just how the end will come.

In the old days when I lived in New England, it used to be quite a habit among some of the dear old ladies to show one quite a little outfit of frocks which they had prepared for their exit from this earth!

To me there is something pitifully sad about this attitude, because it is such a reflexion on the human mind. It is such an insult to the dignity of the soul. It is such a denial of man's highest hopes and aspirations.

Let us have common sense and illumination enough to believe that we are something more than we seem, and that in the wonderful universal Scheme of Life there is a great destiny in which we are to be very active, in which we are to live and work, fully conscious of our own essential divinity.

One of the greatest secrets of life is for a man to believe in his own divine qualities, in his power to surmount all difficulties and to overleap all conditions — especially to overleap the irrational and gloomy picture of death which so many people hold.

How readily one can conceive that from those who are conscious of their own essential divinity the Voice of the Soul is heard! And while this voice should not be taken for the voice of the Great Universal Soul, it is at least an echo of it, a reflexion or ray of it, so to speak.

We must begin early to teach our children

The Beauty of a Perfect Life the idea of the eternity of the spiritual soul, the divinity of the real man, and remove from their minds the horrible harrowing picture of death and funerals.

Let us teach humanity the true story of Nature; that when the body dies — being physical and material and of the earth only,— all that belonged to the body returns to its material elements; but the well-spring of man's being, the enlightener, the invigorator, the great life-giving urge, the spiritual soul, is part of Eternity and cannot die, but goes on and on upon its evolutionary journey. Nature is very gentle and kind and allows us to leave behind us all sad memories.

There is a mightiness in the thought of the spiritual power of even one single human being in this world, and greater mightiness in the thought of the thousands who are all moving on, though, alas! as yet unacquainted with their spiritual heritage.

But in spite of all our aspirations, we still move on with our eyes downwards. We do not keep them up to the grand possibilities of another life and of still other lives. We do not look out into the future and visualize the possibilities of a man who wins his victory, not only with one or another kind of self-control, but of one who finds his true place where he can shine out in the glory of his life and send back to us the story of the beauty of a perfect life!

And how easy it is to attain! How much sweeter would human life be, if we could only fulfill our missions here! How much happier we should all be! How much better we could then all keep united and live out our lives to the fullest point of perfection for this one life!

We are not declaring the glory of the spiritual soul until we can stand upright and recognise our superb possibilities and future.

There is so much meaning in some of the very smallest things we do. But we do not often speak of or believe in their importance until they come home to us on such an occasion as the parting with our loved ones.

Each one evolves according to his understanding of the facts of Nature and according to his education and his environment; so each has his own way of learning, which is different from that of everyone else, because no two have evolved to an equal degree.

The Eternal Fulfilment of the Law

The beauty of Reincarnation is that it gives every man another chance. I repeat this over and over again: it is one of the brightest and most beautiful doctrines that I have ever been able to present to anyone, even to the condemned in prison: yes, there is another chance for all.

The Laws of the Universe or 'the laws of God' are eternal and universal. One cannot escape them. Try, therefore, to reach a conception of the spiritual life and then apply it to the daily life. It means nothing unless it is applied. Carry with you every day as you go through life the idea of the eternal fulfilment of the law and man's perfectibility.

Only those who hear the truth from the Voice of the Soul can understand these things and apply them fully; yet they are so simple that a child can comprehend them in degree.

Unexpected things must evolve where

there is a body united in a grand purpose, in universal, unselfish purposes. Something must be growing, something more than you can say or do, something within the air, from the very Source of Life, the great wonder of life, that inexpressible Source and Center where we sometimes go in our silent moments. It is to me very truly a fact that something then happens, that something noble then grows out of our natures; we cannot describe it; we can hardly echo it; but somehow it has come to stay. We shall find new light and new life, and a better understanding, a sweeter and nobler unity, and more comprehension.

Soul-Power

It is the unspeakably beautiful things in the simple efforts of noble living that make life possible. When we do our duty well and we have the opportunity to gather about us those who love us, we mark time for some new and splendid events.

Be willing to struggle, if there is struggle; be willing to be disappointed, and be willing to suffer and be willing to be misunderstood —

The Value of Life and the Soul's Opportunities

anything in the world that will give you the chance to throw away all personality and bring home to yourself the realization that Soul-power is the only thing that will make life livable.

We have only to think just a little deeper and look a little farther away from our personalities, and take into our understanding the grand and royal and sublime examples we have had in H. P. Blavatsky and William Q. Judge, to realize the mightiness of life and to feel our closer association with the higher possibilities in our own natures, and a rising quality of sincerity.

This is what is needed more than anything else to awaken humanity to deeper thinking and to a realization that man is in essence a mighty creature; and that a human being with all his possibilities, with all that Nature has given him and with all that lies within the soul, is afforded rich gifts continuously.

As we push forward, as we think more deeply, as we enlarge our conception of life, and our conception of duty and grow ever nearer to its fulfilment, we challenge ourselves again and again. It is beautiful to think that we are ready, that we have the opportunity of challenging ourselves.

I wonder if all of us attempt to reach sufficiently towards the depths of our natures in one lifetime ever to keep on doing, to persevere, and to hold firmly in the spirit of the nobler efforts? Thus we cannot fail to push forward with more trust and more confidence in the larger life; and in this determined push, throw ourselves out to what seems impossible to our human minds now. If we do this, we shall have a key that will open the door to such splendid and undreamed of realities for us before we go on to another life, that we shall surely think we have passed through several incarnations in one!

We have our hearts touched very deeply when we undergo the experience of the passing away of those whom we love dearly. There are always compensations, of course, in the thought that they have gone to a condition that is better for them,— to a larger development. But we should also stop and realize that there is then a sacred demand made upon us to cancel our indebtedness not only to humanity but to the Divine Law working for us and in us in this earth-life.

This brings me again to the subject of the value of life. In view of all that happens to us, and all that we see, and know, and feel, and desire, we ought to realize that we have a duty that is so sacred that it would be cowardly to turn away from it. We must answer the challenge and realize the soul's possibilities. We must step out and daily do our grand and superb duties in such a way that the history of our Theosophical Work in after years will be a revelation to those that follow.

We are not working just for today or tomorrow, but we are working for all the days to come and the months to come and for the people to come, and for the souls that will return here. So take hold of the Now as a great omen, a very splendid promise that has come from somewhere, we need not question how, to bring us to the point of awakening where we shall find ourselves fully alive, fully up to our duty, and full of that great love which the Higher Law demands.

Inner Illumination

Man undervalues himself. I do not mean in the worldly sense, but in the spiritual sense. He undervalues his own inner nature. He undervalues his responsibilities, and therefore he is very apt to undervalue his neighbors.

If, on the other hand, he begins to value his inner life and the spiritual side of his being, he is bound to reach a quality of his nature that will bring him to more conscientious thought of his neighbors.

Pursuing this line farther, we shall find ourselves working out a grand scheme of justice for all men to each other; and we shall begin to have some idea of the splendid promises that are written in every moment of our lives.

The consciousness of real manhood and womanhood we must have, if we are to do justice to our Cause, justice to our Theosophical

Work, and justice to the purpose of our lives.

We do not have to follow beaten tracks in any of our efforts to help humanity. We must begin in a new way. We need to think of the new-born day. We need the new-born man and woman, the new-born hope, and the new-born promises. We need many things which we have not, because we do not reach out for them.

Nothing is more pitiful and more shocking to me than to find a person so tied up in his selfish personality that he cannot move outside of his own narrow horizon. This to me is committing a crime against the Holy of Holies in oneself.

Men look upon life too lightly. They lack that deeper and more serious tone that must come into their lives if they are ever to reach those higher levels of self-directed evolution which Theosophy has made possible for humanity.

The preciousness of the moments lies not so much in the actual physical work that one does, but rather in feeling through

INNER ILLUMINATION

every fiber of our being something that will strike a higher note for a brighter tomorrow.

It is essential that we attend to the small things in life — the small duties and responsibilities, and the small demands that are made upon us by the very laws of our being. The seemingly small things in my life have often led to the greatest opportunities. It is often the small things that carry us to our goal.

My endeavor is to give you a conception of the importance of a man's life when he has found that he has an inner nature, and that it is wholly dependable; that he has within himself those rare and wonderful resources for self-restoration, so to speak. In the inner chambers of our natures there are wonderful mysteries. If we could fathom these, we should have a true companionship with the inner Self, and that inner Self is of abiding, eternal character.

Do not try to fashion yourselves like others. Dare to think sufficiently long and sufficiently deeply to receive a revelation from within. Make clean self-analysis a regular habit. Take ten minutes with yourself every day and absolutely surrender your mental self to your Higher Self. Then you will open for yourself a book of revelations.

The Kingdom of Heaven Within

I assume that everyone is at times touched with unhappiness. But the shadows and the disappointments will stay by you and they will grow, and you cannot undo them until you find within yourself the key, the energy, and the inner enlightenment and inspiration that come from a man knowing himself and bringing himself to the point of adjustment where he is willing to face the world with a quality of optimism such as only the Theosophists have.

Bring humanity into this state of mind, and then think of the possibilities of motherhood, and of the possibilities of the children! Then think of the possibilities of eternal life — of never-ending progress towards an ever-expanding perfection through many lives!

Even if one does not believe in Reincarnation, that does not make it untrue.

One may not find it out until, in a sense, it is too late — until he passes on. But the teaching takes nothing from you and it gives everything to you; and it is as old as the ages and has stood the fiery test of time.

If you spend all your time thinking of the outer aspects of life, of this one little earth-life: if you keep away from the largeness of your own inner nature, if you have no faith in your essential divinity and no trust in it, the light is not with you. Consequently you lose the things that you really most need.

These things of the spirit are greater than all the money or success that can come to you, and greater than all the outward facts of your existence, because they touch your inner nature.

I am not telling you anything new. All the greatest teachers, and savants, and writers, who have attempted to do anything really good for humanity, have taught of the inner life of man. Jesus in his time, and to the people he taught, did so as fully as others.

Are we not looking for something better than what we have now? Have you all found happiness? Have you all found your places in life? Are you satisfied with life as it is? Are you ready to go on and on and see children born in ignorance, unwise marriages and tragic divorces, and murders and unnamable crimes sweeping in to the very threshold of your own homes, and not turn for knowledge to these higher laws?

Certainly something is lacking; and that lack can be met by each of us, if we can have courage enough to believe that we are something more than what we seem in our merely physical aspect; that we are a part of the divine Scheme of Life, and that we have within us those latent powers which Jesus referred to when he told us that the Kingdom of Heaven is within us. Interpreted Theosophically, that is a magnificent teaching for helping humanity.

You may have glimpses of a solution of life's problems in your own mental attitudes; you may have touches of it in your hearts; but the world does not propose — according to our present form of civilization — so-called — that you shall grow spiritually.

Life a Superb Challenge

The general opinion of mankind today is that man is weak, vacillating, and has no spiritual basis upon which to work. But Theosophy steps to the front and says: While it is true that we are all subject to the laws of change in evolution, still, life is a superb challenge if one knows how to meet it.

The idea that man is born in sin and is helpless is nonsense. There is nothing reasonable in it. The teaching of Theosophy, on the contrary, which every noble-minded man and woman must ultimately entertain, is that man is essentially divine, that he is a part of the Eternal Plan, and has within himself the key to the mysteries of the Universe and therefore of his own nature; if he hasn't it consciously, he should find it: Theosophy gives it.

I do not talk very much about humility. I do not believe that a man or a woman should be humble in the ordinary sense.

On the other hand, I believe that they should find the strength of their own characters. They should analyse themselves cleanly, find out whence they came, what they are here for, and what life means. They should challenge themselves and move away from the nonsense that they have been taught for so long about being such dreadful sinners. Move out into a great world of superb thought and universal ideas!

If a man lose faith in himself, can one expect him to believe in his neighbor? After all these ages of a certain quality of education that has been given us from childhood, we still have not our hands on the oars that will carry our boat into port.

If we are not sure of our spiritual immortality, if we are not sure of the divine life within us, we cannot live it and we cannot act in accordance with it, though it is there. The inner life is the real life.

When you come to the point where your bodies are tired and you are ready to throw off the worn-out overcoat of flesh,

LIFE A SUPERB CHALLENGE 69

then the truth will be revealed to you. But by that time you are speechless in what the world calls death, but which Theosophy calls rebirth.

The revelation of these inner mysteries can come only to those who will receive them; yet every man and every woman can have glimpses of the truth, day by day, and hour by hour, without price. Spiritual truths are not purchasable.

You are either going up or you are going down. You do not ever stand still. You are something more than you seem.

Love is the greatest power in the world, and self-control is the magic talisman. With love in our hearts, and self-control, we are on the path that leads to the relative perfection of man.

Mere reason and brain-mind arguments keep humanity away from the richness of the inner life that belongs to all. When you have that truth, you will know how to live; when to speak and when not to speak; when to act and when not to act. You will be so conscious of your essential divinity that you will have the strength to dare to do a thousand things that you thought yourselves incapable of doing. You will remove yourselves from the negative psychology of the age and become characters of true positive nobility. Your whole life depends upon your character.

Continuous and confident virtue comes from the knowledge of one's soul-life. It is the expression of the strength of the inner man — that part of one which does noble things, aspires to do them, and is ever restless until one has done them.

When you find a man of real character in his manhood, and a woman of splendid womanhood, you may then know that they have touched the fringe of Truth. They have in some way, though they may not know it, reached a part of the superb and glorious teachings of the Ancient Wisdom, Theosophy, which H. P. Blavatsky brought to the western world, but which she never originated or invented. She brought them to us that we might learn the importance of character-building in the education of the boys and girls and the young men and women, that they might know their strength, their power to fashion their own characters nobly, and thus live in the perfect confidence of the spiritual life and find the real joy of living. *"Born in Sin" vs. Soul-Courage*

Theosophy teaches that this life really is joy. It is pure joy! Find it!

People do not stop to think how humanity has been psychologized for ages with the old idea that man is 'born in sin.' How much real soul-courage can one expect from a man who is burdened and weighed down with that old dogma and carries it with him night and day — eats with it, sleeps with it, and lives with it? There is degradation and humiliation in it. From these follow lack of courage, lack of confidence, until life seems a farce, if it were not for the tragedies and heartaches everywhere.

If one accepts the idea of only one lifetime, he loses sight of the grandeur and beauty and inspiration of the idea of Eternity.

If man as we know him today is the highest aspect of creation, then it is easy to believe that there has been some mistake made somewhere along the way. For thousands of years these teachings have been instilled into the minds of our ancestors, until we have got the poison of them in our very blood and we carry it in our faces. It has made men timid and doubtful of their own abilities. It has limited the courage of even the bravest heroes and lessened the power of the greatest statesmen and the most splendid men and women who have accepted the idea of man's original sinfulness and the limitation of one earth-life.

On the other hand, let us face the man who knows that he is born under the divine and wonderful laws of nature; whose life is a series of awakenings through babyhood, childhood, boyhood, into manhood, with a consciousness of his own essential divinity.

Now this divinity is not such an abstraction as many imagine. It is not so very far away. To believe that the All-Powerful,

All-Loving, Ever-Serving Center of Light, the Great Source of Life —'God'— has designed or had any part in a work that would bring degradation or despair to 'His' own creation, so to speak, is an insult to our manhood and our womanhood; it is an insult to our time and to our intelligence and to our civilization.

If we could only spend less time talking of men's weaknesses and of our children's weaknesses and move out into the great broad view of life which Theosophy gives! The mother's soul would speak and say, "Nay, never, never was this wonder, this child of mine, this mystery to me and mystery to the world, never was it born in sin! It is only to be explained by accepting the divine laws of Nature; and it came to me for a great purpose. The soul is full of richness, full of possibilities, full of potential qualities, and the Divine is in every man."

If our children could grow in this idea, we might bring our youth up to such a high standard that we should all look at life in an entirely new light. Could it be possible that there would be so many disasters and terrible crimes and shocking evidences of man's inhumanity to man? No, it would not be possible. But we have grown negative; we have lost to a degree — or at least we have overlooked,— the strength of our own souls; the power of the inner life.

Warfare and Brotherhood

In this world of ours, with all our wealth and our great territory and our so-called culture, we cannot honestly call ourselves a civilized people as long as there is even the suggestion of warfare near us, nor so long as there are the dreadful aspects of human depravity which fill our newspapers with the horrors of man's inhumanity to man.

As the days go on, I feel the woes of the world, so to speak. And my only consolation is to think: Well, even if I have only done a little and I have done it well, that is better than doing nothing at all. This is why I continue striving, and why I am still here; and I hope that whatever may be said by me you may know that it comes from an honesty of purpose and from a determination to make clear the truths of Theosophy. The will of the writer is to assist humanity to find the secrets of its own life and the panacea for all the ills that afflict human nature; to endeavor to clear the air and purify the thought of men with the idea that man is his brother's keeper. When we reach this point, we shall begin to know something about ourselves and something about the meaning of life.

Setting our Own Houses in Order

Study Theosophy conscientiously and you will find that something is happening in your own nature: you will recover yourself, renovate yourself, readjust yourself, rebuild yourself; and in doing this, you refashion your own character.

I am as certain as I live, that if the teachings of Theosophy were in the homes of all the people of the world, or if even a portion of the doctrines were understood as H. P. Blavatsky attempted to teach them, it would not be long before some of our prison-doors would open; and after a while we would hear less of horrible crimes and less of deathly, unnatural things; — we are having much more of such things since the war. We would have less anxiety about our children. We would have absolute surety about the foundation of our homes; and more than these, we would have a superb trust that would make tomorrow bright.

All will be right if we are right ourselves. But we must be in place. We must meet these teachings at least half-way. We must look at life differently.

If you have no other teacher in the world, study Nature, and Nature will tell you many of these things that Theosophy teaches. She will bring you new life and new light.

I am absolutely assured of the essential divinity in man, of his power to conquer conditions and to make the whole world over again.

I am trying to lift the veil for humanity, to make the vista more beautiful and more encouraging, by ingraining into your minds those great principles of Theosophical optimism upon which I live. I rise with it in the morning; I cannot move away from it; and that is the beauty of living the Theosophical life.

The great key to the solution of life's problems is: "Man, know thyself"; bring thyself to the knowledge of thy essential divinity, of thy strength and thy real purposes and thy hopes and thy visions. The will which makes a man a good man and brings these things into realization is the spiritual will, whereas that will which makes him lose his way, is the will of the personality, of the body only, and dies when the body dies.

In twenty years from now, when science shall have done more for us, we shall find that we have had more lunatics outside the insane-asylums than we have had in them.

The great beauty and charm of life is to have knowledge — not just belief and faith. All your disappointments, and trials, and apparent injustices will not disappear immediately, because the basis of most of them was sown by yourselves; but they can be so well understood and so intelligently met, that you can rise above them and soar beyond them, and bring out before the world the richer and deeper meaning of your life.

Even the most critical savants today in studying H. P. Blavatsky's books, particularly *The Secret Doctrine*, are amazed at the depth and the breadth of her knowledge. They cannot understand or explain where she found it. It is marvelous!

There is nothing in Theosophy to carry one outside the world of reasonable thought. It keeps one on middle lines; not going to extremes; no fanaticism, no nonsense; none of the stuff that some of these people who call themselves theosophists have been talking about in connexion with a 'coming Christ,' and all sorts of rubbish — not at all! The Theosophy which H. P. Blavatsky brought involves common sense applied to human needs.

When she came to America she did not know what would be the attitude of mind of very many people, who represented conventional religion, towards any innovations. So, although in time her work had a magnificent triumph, in the beginning it was decided by those who wrote her up in the newspapers, that she was an impostor, a charlatan, and that she was fanatical and queer, and perhaps somewhat dangerous!

So one can readily imagine that her ideas of the freedom and liberality of the American people suffered quite a shock after she had been here a short time and read the prejudiced accounts of her own life in newspapers from north, south, east, and west, which heaped upon her obloquy and ridicule. That was the reception she received in America.

I have had quite as warm receptions in different parts of Europe as H. P. Blavatsky received in my own country. But, as with her, my enthusiasm has carried me through.

It is a mighty thing to know that there are laws, so infinitely and divinely true and just that if we will reach out to them in aspiration, we can find ourselves in a new world of thought; and when we are discouraged or despairing, we can fill our lives with a royal optimism; for we can take in the grandeur, the beauty, the mercy, and, above all, the superb justice of life.

We can look into our own hearts and go back to the aspirations of our youth, when we were trying to do some of the grand things that earth-life offers us opportunity to do, and we move away from the limited conception of one short life on earth and see the vision of another chance, and another chance, in repeated incarnations.

The students connected with the work at our International Headquarters and the members identified with the Universal Brotherhood and Theosophical Society throughout the world, are very much in earnest.

There are no salaries to be earned in our Organization, no selfish honors to win, nothing but the consciousness of having found the great opportunity of knowing Theosophy and of applying it to their lives, of moving out into a world of thought that all people need, and of giving this message, simple as it is, to tired humanity, with an earnestness and a spirit of devotion that bespeak the truth of what we say. When they find this, then they have some hope for the future, for themselves, for their children, and for the world.

Râja-Yoga

In studying some of the Eastern literature, I discovered the name 'Râja-Yoga'— a Sanskrit word meaning literally 'Kingly Union,' and signifying the perfect balance of all the faculties, physical, mental, and spiritual; and as this expressed the ideal of the school that I was about to found, I gave to it this name.

There was one thing I found when a child; and that is, that we must live and let live. I believed then in evolution, although I did not clearly define it; but I knew that we had all developed in different degrees and under different circumstances. And Nature to me was always so beautiful, and love was so grand and superb. 'God' was in everything — in the song of the birds, in the voice of the waters nearby, and in the cold winds as they swept in from the sea. All these things used to talk to me.

I discovered even as a child that the essential need of humanity is a deeper expression of love for every human being. I grew up in this thought, living in a little world of my own; but my opportunity to declare myself did not come until I met, under very remarkable circumstances, William Quan Judge, who was H. P. Blavatsky's Successor as Leader and Teacher in the Theosophical Movement. He was born in Ireland and educated as a lawyer. He had met her as a young man and became deeply interested in this philosophy which she brought.

He told me of H. P. Blavatsky, who had already passed away, and showed me her book called *The Secret Doctrine*. I was then grown to womanhood, and when I read that wonderful book, and later read her other books, that woman's life became to me a glorious and sacred memory, that had come out of the past and would stay with me forever. It fired my blood, warmed my heart; and stirred my mind all these years under persecution, in order that I might tell my story

RÂJA-YOGA 83

to the world. And that is how at last I came to found the Râja-Yoga School at Point Loma.

The secret of the Râja-Yoga system, for those who know how to apply it, is: gentleness, kindness, firmness, never allowing a child to give way to a temper or to have its own way in anything that is wrong, but patiently helping it to see what is right and directing its energies into useful channels. Cross words on the part of the teachers are not allowed; and never are the pupils punished.

Even our little ones of six and seven years of age very soon learn that they have two natures, and they can and do explain in a rather wise way, yet very childishly and beautifully, the difference between these two natures. We strive never to ingrain into them any ideas that will overstrain them. We keep them close to Nature. They grow up just like the flowers grow, under wise supervision.

The Râja-Yoga education, among other things, gives to the child an opportunity *to find itself*, and to find true knowledge within itself.

SECTION II

Helena Petrovna Blavatsky

"*He who hearing his brother reviled and, keeping a smooth face, leaves the abuse unnoticed, tacitly agrees with the enemy as if he admitted the same to be proper and just. He who does it is either mouse-hearted, or selfishness is at the bottom of his heart. He is not fit as yet to become a 'Companion.'*"

— FROM THE ANCIENT TEACHINGS

HELENA PETROVNA BLAVATSKY

A Brief Sketch of her Life and of her Mission

I RECALL my first knowledge of Helena Petrovna Blavatsky, this Russian noblewoman of marvelous spiritual power, who founded the Theosophical Society in New York in 1875. Beyond all question, she had a great inner spiritual urge.

There was something very remarkable about this woman; and I really think that it would be a great injustice to her and possibly also an injustice to you, if I did not tell you something about her. Many Theosophists seem to be afflicted with a sort of half-timidity or over-modesty in proclaiming their wonderful truths; and I perhaps have been one such myself in some ways.

I feel sure that the more you know of H. P. Blavatsky and the more you discover and discern of her life, her character, and her

A Russian Noblewoman of Marvelous Spiritual Power

teachings, the more will you come to the same conclusion that I have found inescapable; and that is, that she herself was a convincing proof of the doctrine of Reincarnation; because it was utterly impossible that the knowledge which she possessed and which her books demonstrate could have all been acquired in one short lifetime.

"The Greatest Spirit of the Nineteenth Century"

A noted German critic, Karl Bleibtreu, speaks of her greatest work, *The Secret Doctrine*, as "a revealing deed — a compendium of unparalleled knowledge in various branches of science still more marvelous."

I advise those who are unfamiliar with her teachings, to read first her *Key to Theosophy*, which was written by her for inquirers. There are other books also and a large number of articles written by her. They all reveal the woman and the motive and purpose of her life.

Her work was truly a phenomenal one and must appeal to every intelligent human being who has the welfare of humanity at heart. I have known many former materialists, who have changed about from their set and limited view of life simply through studying H. P. Blavatsky's writings; they found therein the key of life. So it is of her that I shall speak.

H. P. Blavatsky and W. Q. Judge

Much has been written about her childhood, and I received a great deal of direct information from William Quan Judge, my predecessor, who succeeded H. P. Blavatsky as Leader and Teacher of the Theosophical Movement throughout the world. He knew her better than any other person with whom she was associated, and she expressed complete confidence in him at all times.

The following is quoted from an official letter written by her to the Convention of the Theosophical Societies in America in 1888:

"To WILLIAM Q. JUDGE, General Secretary of the American Section of the Theosophical Society:

"My dearest Brother and Co-founder of the Theosophical Society:

"In addressing to you this letter, which

I request you to read to the Convention summoned for April 22nd, I must first present my hearty congratulations and most cordial good wishes to the Society and to yourself — the heart and soul of that body in America.

"We were several to call it to life in 1875. Since then you have remained alone to preserve that life through good and evil report. It is to you chiefly, if not entirely, that the Theosophical Society owes its existence in 1888.

"Let me thank you for it, for the first, and perhaps for the last time publicly and from the bottom of my heart, which beats only for the cause you represent so well and serve so faithfully.

"I ask you also to remember that, on this important occasion, my voice is but the feeble echo of other more sacred voices, and the transmitter of the approval of Those whose presence is alive in more than one true Theosophical heart, and lives, as I know, pre-eminently in yours."

Further, H. P. Blavatsky, in December

of the same year, wrote the following:

"As Head of the Esoteric Section of the Theosophical Society, I hereby declare that William Q. Judge of New York, U. S. A., in virtue of his character as a disciple of thirteen years' standing and of the trust and confidence reposed in him, is my only representative for said Section in America, and he is the sole channel through whom will be sent and received all communications between the members of the said Section and myself, and to him full faith, confidence, and credit in that regard are to be given."

On October 23, 1889, H. P. Blavatsky wrote:

"The Esoteric Section and its life in the U. S. A. depend upon W. Q. Judge remaining its agent and what he is now. The day W. Q. Judge resigns, H. P. Blavatsky will be virtually dead for the Americans."

H. P. Blavatsky's early childhood was in some ways not unlike many other children's

H. P. Bla-vatsky's Childhood

of her station in life. She was born in 1831 of a very distinguished family at Ekaterinoslaff, Southern Russia. She was the daughter of Colonel Peter Hahn, and of Helena Fadeyef. On her father's side, she was granddaughter of General Alexis Hahn von Rottenstern Hahn (the representative of a noble family of Mecklenburg, Germany, settled in Russia). On her mother's side, she was the grand-daughter of Privy-Councillor Andrew Fadeyef and of the Princess Helena Dolgoruky.

Her family were known for their patriotism and their great ability along literary and other cultural lines. They were very humane and unusually broad-minded.

Helena's earliest childhood tells of nothing remarkable. But as she grew older, she was full of questions. The most interesting thing about her questions is that they were frequently of a kind that her parents and governesses could not answer. She would then often surprise her elders by answering the questions herself. She was very much sheltered and protected during her tender years and knew very little about life — especially about its suffering and its cruelties.

But at an unusually early age she began to puzzle over the contrasts that she saw in Russia. Why, she asked, were some people happy and others miserable? Why were some poor and others rich? Why was Nature so bountiful and beautiful and yet why were there so many uncertainties and inconsistencies in human life? These questions must have come to her from her own inner perceptions. There is no other way to account for them.

It was very plain to her family that she was an unusual child, and they felt that she was destined to a great career of some kind; but I am certain that they never dreamed what would be the future of their beautiful daughter whom they loved and cared for, not only in the ordinary way that most good parents do, but as a precious being of wonderful promise.

Her first experience that is recorded as

Her Spiritual Awakening having made an indelible impression upon her, occurred on one of her father's estates. She was very fond of the out-of-doors life and spent much of her time alone in communion with Nature. But on this special occasion she heard dreadful screams and cries of agony, answered by brutal shouts of command. So she rushed over to the side of her father's estate bordering on the roadway, whence the cries of distress were coming. She climbed upon the hedge and looked over. There she beheld a number of prisoners being sent to Siberia in charge of officers who were beating them, dragging them, cuffing them, throwing them down and striking them. Their cries of pain and exhaustion were unavailing.

Now I am told that Helena screamed in horror at the awfulness of the moment, and then fainted.

Mr. Judge assured me that from that time something very remarkable came into her nature. Though previously of a happy and buoyant nature, it is said that she did not smile for months after that time. She

became oppressed with the idea that she was
not in the right place in her beautiful home of *She comes*
wealth and comfort, when elsewhere there was *to America*
suffering. Young as she was — I think she
was then about fifteen — it was very hard for
her parents to keep her from going out into
the world in order better to understand and
thus to lift the burdens of the people.

After a while, following some bitter personal experiences which were forced upon her by her well-intentioned relatives, she set out upon her world-travels at her father's expense, in search of truth and in search of some explanation for the world's suffering and some remedy for it. She visited nearly all the countries of the world. In 1851-2 she was in America for about a year.

Without following in detail her many travels in Europe, Asia, Africa, and America — all the way from Tibet to Cairo and Canada, and from Java to England and Mexico — I will skip to the early seventies, when she came again to New York imbued with a spirit of helpfulness that became more and more apparent as time went on; and with a determination of will that was iron in its power.

Here was a noblewoman of unusual refinement but with little knowledge of the English language, with very limited financial means, because, as she drew away from the worldly life which her family had intended for her, their support of her became less and less, until it ceased altogether; so she had to pull along as best she could.

But think of the vision that she must have had at that time in her love of humanity and in her faith in the infinite power of the inner life! Think of the trust that she must have had in the Higher Law, and the confidence that she had in the strength of her own soul! There must have opened to her inner eyes a wonderfully beautiful and uplifting vista, which gave her the never-failing enthusiasm that she was noted for.

She came to America with almost a childlike confidence in 'the land of the free'! But she had scarcely touched our shores before she found that newspapers all over the country were alive with the spirit of persecution against her. I have the files of many of these periodicals; and they are a living disgrace to our 'free America.' It is a dreadful record of narrow-minded persecution.

She had not come to America to meddle with our politics; nor did she come to disturb anybody who was sincere in his religious convictions. All she asked was the opportunity to come to this 'land of liberty' and deliver her message. She said that she had one, and we all know now that she did have one, and it was very simple. It was nothing that she had invented or fabricated or anything of that sort. She did not claim it as her own, but emphatically said that it was the Ancient Wisdom and as old as thinking man.

One cannot tell what her vision was, nor what the many visions were that she had in making this great effort. But there was something in her life that showed that she would not live very long and that she must accomplish a great deal in a short time, if she was

Founding of the Theosophical Society

to fulfil her great mission. She aimed to spread her message — the sacred teachings of Theosophy — all over the world, and she chose this country to launch it in, because, as I have said, she thought that here there was more of the spirit of liberty, more progress, more open-mindedness.

Imagine her disappointment when she found that scarcely a day passed that the newspapers did not contain not only criticism but the most outrageous and ridiculous charges. She was accused of being a charlatan, an impostor, and all that sort of thing.

But the remarkable thing is that she never faltered; she never turned back. And yet this is not so remarkable to one who knows her as I feel that I do, though I have no personal memory of her. As a matter of fact it was impossible for her to give up what she had started out to do.

She founded the Theosophical Society in New York in 1875. She wrote and she traveled all over this country — and later throughout the world. In less than a year she had gathered into her thought-atmosphere, into her heart-life, and into the sphere of her influence, of her energy, of her wisdom, and of her intense yearning for the salvation of humanity, some really wonderful people. Many of them represented the best intellects and the most honorable and dignified lovers of humanity in this country.

Her Message

The Theosophical Society was soon known all over the world. It is now called the Universal Brotherhood and Theosophical Society, which is nearer to what she at first wished to call it than merely 'The Theosophical Society.'

H. P. Blavatsky's message teemed with a spiritual virility that we are all hungry for, because it is something that the whole world is seeking and has not yet found. She presented her message in the simplest and most beautiful way. Her logic is unanswerable. I challenge you to read her books, not just for your entertainment, but perhaps in order to prove that she was wrong.

I have yet to find one competent person whom I have directly challenged in this way, who has accepted the challenge and then has declared that she was wrong. On the contrary, after studying H. P. Blavatsky's writings, these critics have turned towards our philosophy and have found in it new life and new hope.

And this is also the reason why I am here: to accentuate certain Theosophical principles that would cause my listeners to dig down into the deeps of their natures and find this new life and this new hope, which not only their minds but their very souls crave. No one can question that the world needs just this message, and needs it badly.

The influence of Theosophy is spreading very rapidly; the teachings which H. P. Blavatsky brought to the western world are now known and understood by thousands everywhere. They are the essential truths of life that were forgotten, almost thrown aside, in the past, especially since the beginning of the Christian era. They were supposed to be out of place, because they gave man too much liberty of thought; they taught him that he was essentially a divine soul instead of a miserable sinner; that he was free to make his own destiny, to adjust his own future, to make of his life a blessing or a blasphemy, to create his own heaven or his own hell.

With an understanding of H. P. Blavatsky's message comes the blessed realization of the lifting of a heavy weight from the heart, of the dispelling of the shadows that are over our unfortunate humanity, groping to find its way, to raise the veil, and crying in its despair: "O ye gods, open the way that we may know!"

But the answer, though always there, was not recognised until H. P. Blavatsky brought it and taught it openly.

The more you study her teachings, the more you will realize their antiquity, and the more you will appreciate the vast possibilities of human life; because, I repeat, she accentuated above everything the fact of man's essential divinity. If she had done nothing more than this, if she had passed away without writing a single one of her great books, she would have performed a wonderful service for man's spiritual liberation in emphasizing that one doctrine and fact of being.

The Spreading of Theosophy

The philosophy which H. P. Blavatsky brought has slowly made its way into the hearts of the people of America and of all other countries: especially since the world-war has there been a manifestation of unusual interest in the teachings of Theosophy.

The war ushered us into a questioning age. Before that time many people went through life without serious thought of any kind. They questioned very little; they accepted what they were told or what they read; they looked upon this one earth-life as all there was to existence; they were not very sure about the tomorrow, and did not concern themselves much with it. So spiritually they did not grow; they did not inwardly expand; they did not enlarge their vision; and many lived without hope.

But Theosophy brings even to the most hopeless, the most doubting, and the most uncertain, absolute facts about himself and the world he lives in. If one cannot take them in quickly and with enthusiasm, one will nevertheless find, if he studies them at all carefully, that he will be completely overcome by the wonderful logic used by that great Russian woman in presenting these truths so that they might be accepted.

Man's Essential Divinity

I love to think of what the inner life of that woman must have been.

We all know a great deal about the outer life of people. The material existence of everyone is very much in evidence. We all have the bread-and-butter question to solve. But there are not so many, I think, who have that inner knowledge which comes from a real consciousness of better things or from a recognition of the fact that man's spiritual soul is immortal.

So, as I have often said before, it is a wonder to me how men stand on their feet at all and how human beings hold together even as well as they do without destroying one another.

What is it that preserves humanity? It is that spiritual part of us, that divine spark — not very active in most of us, but still our inspiration; and it is that essential divinity in all men that keeps humanity from destroying itself.

Let us be thankful that we have not all lost our consciences yet; for just as long as the conscience is recognised and followed, there is always human growth and betterment. But unless we have the teaching of the spiritual nature of man as the basis for our conduct, I do not see how we can possibly reason ourselves into any state of real inner peace.

One might think that in saying this I was urging people to throw aside their own spiritual beliefs that are acceptable to them; but it is not so; for it is only the forms, the methods, the dogmas, and the falsehoods which have sprung up among the followers of the great World-Teachers that have obscured and undermined the beautiful truths which they gave to humanity.

The effort of H. P. Blavatsky and the effort of all true Theosophists is to bring home to man the consciousness of his essential divinity, of his spiritual possibilities, and of those potent qualities within him that come from the divine side of his nature, which give him the power to discern the right from the wrong, to know when to speak and when not to speak. The intuitional powers of humanity must develop before we can expect to have better conditions in life.

The timid, frightened, 'miserable-sinner' conception of human life has ruled men long enough! What has Theosophy to offer in its place? More than all else it has the ennobling and inspiring teaching that man is essentially divine; and it shows how his divine nature does evolve forth, and thus causes him to grow, to progress, through different earth-lives!

How can we talk usefully of our aspirations, of our loves, of our devotion to principle, of anything permanent, so long as we accept the old idea that life on earth is limited to seventy-seven or a hundred years, more or less?

Reincarnation

But once accept the doctrine of Reincarnation, and we are conscious of having found an inner anchorage. When we have this, all the rest will be revealed — not written in golden letters and big tablets on the wall, but right in our hearts, in our minds, in our own characters. Then all the questions that are now so puzzling will be revealed and answered — although not in a day, nor even in one lifetime completely.

When a man recognises his own essential divinity, and trusts in it, he will understand the law of evolutionary progress. He will find himself every day knowing a little more. He will advance in self-directed evolution on lines of least resistance.

Even what H. P. Blavatsky openly taught must be very little in comparison with what is known by one who advances and advances through many lifetimes, climbing and climbing ever nearer to the goal of perfection. That is the beauty of the teachings of Theosophy. One's aspirations grow ever higher and higher; the light comes into the soul, and man finds the Kingdom of Heaven in splendor. Did not Jesus say the Kingdom of Heaven is within you? Who will contradict him?

We Theosophists look upon Jesus just as H. P. Blavatsky did. We do not accept him as being born in an especial way, but we do accept him as a great Teacher, a great Initiate, a Helper and Savior for the people of his time. We love him and we love his teachings.

Theosophy has taught us very clearly how to discriminate between what Jesus did teach, and what some of his followers have since taught in his name. His actual teachings are so Theosophical that we cannot move away from them. They are eternal verities. Earnest people everywhere, even non-Christians, can accept these. But not the dogmas that have been fashioned about him. And yet, even among professed Christians, probably more than half of them are in doubt, though there are very many well-meaning, noble, and splendid people in their ranks.

"Touching the Fringe of Truth"

Think what Reincarnation will bring to you! It is a key that will open the doors to reality. Study it for yourselves! You need no teacher; you need no revelation; you need no savant to instruct you. Just find the understanding of it within yourself!

All the deeper spiritual things that your souls have been yearning and craving and aching for are right within yourselves. But how to find them? — that is the great secret which Theosophy offers you. It is a matter that is not to be argued about at all. It comes about in mysterious ways.

Perhaps I can best describe what I mean in this manner: Many of our greatest artists have begun very early in their lives merely with a tendency towards artistic productions. After a while they astonish the world with some wonderful achievement. Later, great masterpieces are created and the artists win renown. And yet they have but touched the fringe of truth. Somewhere or somehow they have received inspiration. It did not come from the brain-mind but from the truly spiritual part of man's nature. Then behold! — a work of genius!

The Appeal of Theosophy

Spiritual knowledge manifests itself in all real artistic creation. You will find it everywhere. Whenever art is not up to its highest standards, you will find that the one great secret that is lacking is knowledge of man's own essential divinity, which brings him into his own.

Believing of course as we do in evolution, it is not to be expected that we shall all be artists. We all begin our present earth-lives under certain hereditary conditions and environments, which affect very largely our degree of evolutionary progress. Yet we can, through the mercy of the Higher Law, or through the courage of our own hearts and hands, swing into line with Theosophy.

We Theosophists alone cannot adjust the terrible conditions that confront us today. But we can begin to open the way, to plow through the doubts and the fears and the mistakes of mankind, reach out our hands to all, even to the most wretched; we can sow the seed of brotherhood and implant it in the minds of men, so that ere long the whole psychological nature of humanity will change.

The psychology of this age is death to the soul of man. Yet it is not the product of this age alone. It has passed down through the ages from our ancestors, and there is no other power but Theosophy that can overcome it. It is everywhere. The thought-atmosphere of the world is filled with it.

It seems to me that the more humanity suffers, the more does it turn to added misery, rather than turning towards the light which would reveal the meaning of life. This is not far-fetched.

I am striving to interest you sufficiently so that you will look into Theosophy and challenge it, if you will. No Theosophist would ever attempt to 'convert' you, as this word is generally understood, for we do not believe in such conversion. The only conversion, if it may be so called, that we accept, takes place when a man accepts a truth and makes it a part of his own nature, his own character, his innermost being. Ordinary 'conversion' is often the result of emotion rather than of thought.

The essential thing is to find yourself. Find yourself and you will have the key to life's mysteries, and that key will be Theosophy — pure Theosophy, mind you, not the pseudo-Theosophy that deals in psychic phenomena and other forms of extreme nonsense which impair the intellects of men and obscure the truth.

Theosophy is aiming to clear the way and to bring home to man his divine right, which is the knowledge of his spiritual heritage. In that state of mind life is beautiful and joyful.

Some people think it is sacrilegious and sinful to be happy! Well, we Theosophists are not happy over the condition of the world; yet we are happy in spite of it, because we rejoice over the good karma that gave us the opportunity to discover the glorious teachings of Theosophy and to find out for ourselves the fact of man's essential divinity and the truth of Reincarnation, and to pass it on to others.

Real Theosophy brings joy; it brings hope; it brings knowledge; it brings truth; and with all these things, it brings peace. If each one who receives these teachings holds to them faithfully, and works continuously for human betterment, in time we may have the kingdom of Heaven on earth, which has been promised to us by Jesus and all the great World-Teachers.

If you wish to find inner peace; if you wish to breathe the fresh air of spiritual knowledge into your souls; and if you wish to live a new life tomorrow, have the courage to look into Theosophy and challenge its teachings. The first book you should read is not H. P. Blavatsky's monumental work, *The Secret Doctrine*, but her simpler book for inquirers, *The Key to Theosophy*. There she declares herself; there she tells you who she is, and what she is aiming to do. She calls black black, and white

white; and above all things she gives to man a confidence born of knowledge — a confidence which he must have before he can call himself a man in the truest sense.

SECTION III

An Incident of the First Theosophical World-Tour 1896-7

"Knowledge is the food of the soul."
— SOCRATES

AN INCIDENT OF THE FIRST THEO-SOPHICAL WORLD-TOUR, 1896-7

A Striking Proof of Reincarnation

I HAVE been importuned by several friends to make a statement at some time in reference to the world-tour of Theosophists which I led around the globe in 1896-7 from New York City. The account of this tour has never been published, aside from sketchy reports sent in to our New York Headquarters while we were on the journey. It was certainly replete with remarkable experiences all along the way.

I have thought that at some future time I might write about it, though I shall shiver a bit from fear of the unthinking criticism that possibly will be aroused by some of the very remarkable stories that would be told.

Recently many of my friends have spoken of this world-tour of 1896-7, and realizing

Meeting with the President of the Khedive's Tribunal

that full justice has never been done to those who assisted me then — there were seven members of my staff who went with me from New York — I think I shall be able to make a very interesting report.

But here I want to refer to an experience that impressed me perhaps more than any other that I had during that tour. It was an incident that among many others absolutely proved to me, and proved to those to whom I told the story, the truth of the doctrine of Reincarnation.

It happened in this way. When in the early part of October, 1896, we left Athens, in Greece,— where very remarkable work had been done by our party during our stay there — after a short drive down to Piraeus, we took a small boat which carried us out to the steamship that was to take us to Egypt.

When I was on deck, and before I could go down to my cabin, I was approached by a gentleman in Oriental dress, who handed his card to me as a representative of the President of the Khedive's Tribunal.

THE PRESIDENT OF THE TRIBUNAL 119

Thereafter I met the President every day during the short trip crossing from Greece to Egypt. He told me many of the experiences that he had had in his official position, and he spoke particularly of a time when his father was the Governor of Thebes, when he himself was twelve or fourteen years of age.

He said that then was the time when the remarkable discovery was made of the tomb of Rameses II, containing not only his mummy, but the mummies of a dozen or more other royal personages of ancient Egypt. The history of that discovery was a most interesting one; and the story as told by this Egyptian gentleman was very graphic. I cannot do full justice to it here; but at least I can tell you some noteworthy features of it.

As I suppose you must know, the history of ancient Thebes was for many centuries a most splendid one. The temples which then were built and which still stand in a more or less ruined condition, are even yet wonderful. Other buildings and houses of which we know something from the sketches of ancient Egyptian life which still remain to us, tell us a little at least of what a great and important city it must have been.

Rameses the Second's Tomb Discovered

Thebes is now but a mass of ruins, a scene of devastation. It was some 3,200 years ago that one of the greatest of the Theban kings, Rameses II, lived.

My distinguished Egyptian fellow-traveler told me that, at the period of which he was speaking, great excitement suddenly spread all over Egypt, because of the finding near Thebes, in a certain part of the province under his father's jurisdiction, of the mummy of Rameses II, which archaeologists had always hoped to find, but which had never been discovered up to that time.

You know that it was an ancient Egyptian custom, after the lapse of a certain number of years, to move the mummies of important personages and of royalty especially, which were held most sacred in those days, to places other than where they had been buried, on account of the fear of tomb-breakers and the desecration of the sleeping dead.

The mummy of Rameses II had never been found; and the following is the story which my Egyptian acquaintance told me of the finding of that mummy at the time when his father was governor of that province.

Two young brothers were one day walking over the plains or fields on the western side of the river Nile, at a place where there was no evidence of even remnants of temples or anything of that sort. They were amusing themselves kicking stones about, when they happened to strike a large one which fell into a bush. Their attention was attracted by a noise that the stone made as they heard it fall into a cavity. So they looked farther into the matter.

After digging around on their knees for some time, they found in looking more closely that they stood at a small opening in a great rock.

The next day they returned with a rope and the older brother went down, while the other held the rope; and after a while the first of them was pulled up by the other and brought with him some of the smaller specimens of the wonderful treasures that he had found. He brought out what he could on his back.

For a month he and his brother secretly returned at intervals to the tomb and gathered together as many of the portable finds as they could, and hid them from everyone. Then the elder brother, carrying his treasures in a bag on his shoulders, would go at different times to Cairo, which was some four hundred miles from there, and in Cairo he managed quietly to dispose of his finds.

Now the following was the manner in which they were found out, and their secret discovered. Near Shepherd's Hotel in Cairo — which was also the hotel where I stayed, when I arrived in that city — there was a spot where two streets ran together, and there stood an old-fashioned building with low eaves — so old that it looked as though it would fall to pieces. It seems that the young man brought his treasures here at midnight in a canvas bag on his back; he would go in through the rear door, and sell them for what he could get for them to the dealer who lived there. The man never asked him any embarrassing questions about them, and sold them to people who were staying at the hotel or elsewhere in Cairo.

The excitement created in the city by the exhibition of these beautiful, genuine antiques in the dealer's windows, I was told, at last attracted the attention of the officials; so the government — not the Turkish government, and not the Khedive's officers, but the British government — followed the matter up. The officials planned to watch this young man, and at last they caught him in the very act of taking his bag of treasures into the back door of the dealer's shop.

He was told that he would have to go to prison for years if he did not tell where he had found the antiques which he had been selling and which he then had in his possession. So he finally told the whole truth, much as I have described it here. Then the government officials went south to Thebes and apprehended the other young man, holding him also. The two brothers were compelled to conduct the officials to the place near Thebes where they had made their discovery. A thorough investigation was then made of all the circumstances.

By referring to my notes I can later give further details of the discovery, which was admittedly one of the most wonderful finds in the history of Egyptian archaeology. Not only was the mummy of Rameses II, one of Egypt's greatest kings, found there in the tomb by those who afterwards investigated, but also the mummies of his wife and his child and of a large number of other Egyptian royalties, as well as mummies of certain ones of his officials.

There seemed to be no limit to the treasures in antiques that were there found. The government took immediate possession of these things, of course; and for various reasons the discoverers of this remarkable treasure-house of ancient mummies and archaeological objects were released.

There was a great deal of talk among the government people as to what they were going to do with the mummy of this famous king. They would not leave it where it was found. Some of the highest officials in this department of the government, and other influential people, declared it should be removed and placed with the mummies of the other kings under immediate governmental supervision and care. For some time the matter was discussed; and at last it was decided that the mummies with the other treasures should be brought down to Cairo and placed in the great governmental museum of Bulaq.

But when they were about to do this, to their amazement the officials found that the proposal to remove these treasures and bring them down to Cairo for safe keeping in the museum there, aroused an unsuspected opposition on the part of the Beduins and other natives who lived along the borders of the Nile. And the most interesting thing about this is that these were not of ancient Egyptian descent, but of Arabian ancestry.

These people declared that the mummies were those of their former great kings, and especially so in the case of Rameses II; that he had lived at such and such a time, and that they felt that they had the right to protest against the sacred body being removed. There were even dangerous symptoms of a local insurrection among these Beduins if the officials persisted in doing what was so strongly opposed.

So some time was occupied in preparing a feasible plan to impress the people peacefully to let them bring the mummies down the Nile.

These people lived in little villages along the Nile. They were poor creatures, struggling to obtain a bare physical existence. Much pity is due to them, battling for a mere livelihood under such distressing circumstances.

The government sent out its messengers from village to village, with a really wonderful pronouncement, which was made, I think, by the Khedive's Tribunal. The people were told that the plan was to show the mummies, and particularly that of Rameses II, the greatest official honors — the same honors, in all essential respects, that were shown to the royal dead three thousand or more years ago. They had a ship built approximating in many respects to the type of one of the old Egyptian Nile-boats. It was said that never had anything been seen in modern times equal to it in magnificence. *Egypt's Great King Honored by Modern Beduins with Ancient Rites*

The plan was that there should be a great pageant; they turned the occasion into a gala-time, devoted to pleasure and bountiful feasting, and so forth. On a special day set apart in honor of the ancient Kings of Egypt, the procession started northward from Thebes.

But the government-people and the archaeologists themselves, as well as others, all wondered and questioned why it was that these modern Beduins and the natives generally, very largely of alien stock, should be satisfied to have such official attention and devotion shown to the mummy of a king of Egypt, who was in no way connected with them or their own ancestry. It was too much for those in charge; they simply could not make it out.

When the time came for the procession northward, and sounds of the old Egyptian music resounded over the Nile, and when that splendid ancient Egyptian ship with all its wonderful appurtenances, its magnificent display of colorings, with the government officials and many invited guests aboard, passed by the various villages along the line of its course down the Nile, the bare-footed Beduins — old women and little children, aged men and the youth, indeed thousands of this class — came down to the banks of the river, and there was a great raising of human voices in salutation to the ancient Theban king.

Then, at a certain time, the music changed to a beautiful doleful strain, more appropriate perhaps for the removal of a king's mummy, which the great crowd on either side of the Nile gazed at in silent admiration — the body of one who had done such great things for his country in his own time.

These Beduins along the banks of the river wept and tore their hair, and they dropped upon their knees. They went through the ceremonies which one reads of in the Egyptian books and sees painted in the tomb-pictures, illustrating the ceremonies used when the ancient Egyptians buried their kings. It is said there never was anything so remarkable in modern Egyptian history.

Upon reaching Cairo, all the great city was lighted up.

As I recall the story, the bodies were brought down about fifteen or sixteen years before I arrived in Egypt on that occasion, which was, as I have already said, in 1896. I was told that there was scarcely any limit to the effect in various ways of the action of these simple natives.

Many of the more open-minded and advanced scholars, who realized the extraordinary significance of this native demonstration, turned their minds to seeking any knowledge with which they were conversant that would explain the incident. "Why," they asked, "should these illiterate people of non-Egyptian ancestry follow out the customs and ceremonies of the ancient Egyptians in honoring their dead?" They found an explanation, or at least could easily have found an explanation, of these things in Theosophy, which many of them at that time knew something of, of course; that is, in the doctrine of Reincarnation.

There was no other explanation that I could give (and this explanation was accepted by many of the scholars of that time), than that the sympathy and the sorrow that these illiterate modern Beduins had manifested, and the determination they had to show honor to the mummies of the ancient monarchs of the land — that all this, I say, was due to the action of sleeping memories of other lives imperfectly coming to the surface in them. It was in some respects the greatest proof that the scholars could have had of the truth of Reincarnation. Many of the people along the Nile believed that King Rameses II was the king of their own ancestors — indeed, that they had themselves lived before in Egypt during his time, and that that was doubtless why they were carried away in their feelings of devotion to his mummy.

I tell you the strange tale in substance as it was told to me by this distinguished gentleman of the highest authority in Egypt, the Minister of the Khedive's Tribunal, who met me on the steamer and was, as said, my fellow-traveler until we reached Alexandria, and who, during that time on the steamer spent many hours in telling me of the soul of the Egyptian people and of their old history. His official position made his words carry great weight. You can depend upon it that his story in all essentials was absolutely authentic.

At that time he looked upon America as a very old country, although new in modern records. I told him that America was indeed very old, in fact older than he imagined.

Egypt Older than India, America Older than Either

I told him that Egypt was older than India of historic periods, and that the results of the excavations of archaeologists in the next quarter century or so would be so marvelous, that America would be proved to be the oldest of all three. There is no question that America as a geological continent is older than Egypt or India. That is a fact; and the wonderful archaeological finds that have been made in recent years, even in the last ten, strongly confirm the statement that in civilization it may also take the senior rank.

The tale that I have told you exemplifies human ignorance on the one hand, and human unrest and pain; and on the other hand the working of the soul of man. We are all the children of the universal life. That is our comfort, and we must understand this truth.

If we as students of human life could place ourselves where we belong in the great Universal Scheme of Existence, the enlightenment that would come to us as a result thereof would so broaden our views as to bring about a veritable transformation within ourselves, thorough, clear, and satisfactory.

The Promise of Reincarnation

What is the explanation of the unrest that the people of the world everywhere feel today? It is the hunger of the soul for more knowledge, for more light, for an explanation of the How and the Why of life. For centuries past the human family has been taught that an individual human life lasts for only about a hundred years, more or less. But within the realms of your own inmost being and in your silent moments, you can find an explanation of things that can come in no other way and that you never had before.

You will find that people have drifted away from and lost sight of some of the great teachings of the Ancient Wisdom, particularly of Reincarnation, which gives man the promise of life after life on earth in which to attain ever higher degrees of perfection. Without egoism or conceit or self-love, the man who faithfully pursues this inward search for light realizes that there is within him more than he had dreamed was possible before.

How can any human being hope to approximate even relative perfection in one short earth-life of about seventy-five years? Why, at that age, most of us are just beginning to read the A B C's of real existence! How little we know of it!

Crime and its Prevention

Turning to the subject of crime and its prevention: If we had the means of carrying on such an investigation, I think we would be able to place the beginning of the criminal instincts which are observed in the prisoners now behind the bars, in pre-natal conditions, in the unrest of the parents also, and in the unrest of the parents' own mothers and fathers: in their strains and anxieties over the dollar-and-cents question and in their longings and their disappointments and their ignorance about the real and the unreal things in life.

Should we be surprised that many of our boys and girls go wrong, and are in prison today, when we realize that they grow up entirely unfamiliar with themselves and their possibilities, and the meaning of life, which after all is the only knowledge worth having? True, many of them have probably had loving care from their parents; but the spiritual life was not understood at all. I repeat the question: Under such conditions, should we be surprised if we find them suddenly *non compos mentis*, though they may seem generally sane?

Looking at the subject in this light, should not our hearts open to a deeper compassion for them? Should we not withhold judgment and say to ourselves: "If I had been born under such circumstances, and had lived in similar environment; if I was spiritually blinded and did not know the way — might not I have found myself in a like position?"

The urge of my heart and of my soul is to bring to people the realization of their responsibility in human life.

The whole of humanity, even the noblest and the best of us, are tainted by the psychology of our age; and this psychology is largely the result of the teachings of past ages, which have caused men to lose faith in themselves instead of enabling them to know themselves. All that is true and noble and beautiful is mirrored at times in the aspirations of our thought-life. But no man can make these aspirations a part of his daily conduct by depending solely on an intellectual grasp of life's meaning. It is utterly impossible until man accepts himself as a being divine in essence.

Let a man hold to this belief for a time, if he cannot reason it out with his brain-mind at once, and after a while his weaknesses will pass away, because he will be above them. He will find a new hope, a broader vista, a larger life. He will do his part to make the world more beautiful and more true. In doing this he climbs; though he suffers he learns; when he falls he rises again and goes on climbing, until he knows the truth; and then the truth will make him free.

Our responsibilities to humanity are so great that we should think three or four times before acting, lest we take a false step.

All Nature about us is filled with beauty; our best thoughts are often inspiring; why then cannot our lives equal our yearnings and our hopes? Because the will of man, depending upon the mentality alone, is too weak to dominate the life. Hence there are so many failures, so many disappointments. That is why our prisons are full. That is why every day we read of new manifestations of crime that twenty years ago we could not have believed possible. These things that now stare us in the face are a terrible commentary on the psychology of the age.

We must go into the arena of new effort, open our eyes wide, throw aside prejudices and opinions, and seek facts. Finding facts we reach the truth, and truth gives us light and illumination; the will is strengthened by the conviction that man is essentially a spiritual being, which is the keynote of the philosophy of Theosophy.

There is a ray of spirituality even in the worst of men; and as long as that ray is present, we can still hope for them.

Another Chance for All

The beauty and the glory and the supreme joy of Theosophy are revealed in the following: It says to every man, even to the lowest and the meanest: "There is another chance!" The state may hang a man; it may keep him in prison for life, helping him to grow worse instead of better, alas! but no one can touch the spiritual soul, because it is eternal. It manifests its splendor just as far as the mind permits it to do so.

I repeat: the charm and the wonder and the comfort of Theosophy shine forth in its teaching that all men have another chance, even the most discouraged, those who have lost faith in humanity, and the injured and the oppressed.

The teachings of Theosophy will make clear the way, will explain all apparent injustices; the twin doctrines of Karma and Reincarnation will answer the most perplexing questions.

Realize that the spiritual soul of man is divine; look for the treasures of heaven within yourself! Cherish all the beautiful thoughts and the deepest yearnings of your soul. See how few of them have been realized. Look at life as it is in its eternity, in its vastness. Know that the soul in its growth is going step by step in self-directed evolution towards the goal of ultimate perfection. Find yourself and find peace!

Reincarnation brings Enlightenment

The subject of Reincarnation is very dear to me. It is one of the cardinal teachings of Theosophy, and it contains in itself the panacea for all the ills of the world. In the first place it offers an explanation of all the apparent injustices of life. It gives to the whole of life an entirely new aspect. One's understanding of life grows and progresses, and becomes richer and more sacred and divine.

The very eagerness and restlessness of human faces tell the story that the heart of man is crying for something all the time: Where is the Truth? Where is the Light? Where can we find the answer to our pains and our agonies and our heartaches? Preachers and teachers may talk to you from Monday morning until Saturday night, but you cannot find that which your soul craves until you yourself work for it. And when you work for it, turn your face towards that which proves itself to be helpful. So I say study the doctrine of Reincarnation.

To accept the idea of more than one life on earth, or even to believe that it may be possible, must necessarily change the whole outlook of one's mind. It will bring something new into the consciousness. But of course the subject must be considered and studied to be understood, just as must any other serious subject. No matter how brilliant a man may be or what abilities he may have, he never goes very far in his knowledge of music, for instance, without application and practice, and without determined will-power. And so it is with this subject.

The doctrine of Reincarnation brings enlightenment to the human mind. It takes man out of his mental imprisonment and holds before him a picture of the eternal verities. It shows that the divine laws that govern us all are of a quality that appeals to our souls as well as to our minds. And our lives should be so tinctured with them, and our minds should be so strongly impressed with them, that, while we do our daily duties down to the very letter, yet the greater joy of living would be in finding the truth and following the path of research — daring to challenge these higher and divine laws about which we know so little.

We have no broad conceptions of the meaning and purpose of life; for if we had, we would not allow conditions to be as they are. We would declare ourselves insane and lost if we were to accept the idea that man is limited to just one short lifetime of seventy-seven or a hundred years on earth, as we know it today.

In saying this, I feel that I am revering the Higher Law that governs this great universe and all the universes and all that goes on in the wonderful mysteries of Nature, more than those who limit human existence to one life. I revere the Universal Law that holds us all in its keeping. I feel a sacred trust in it, and everyone should have that trust.

Let the thoughtful mother not attempt to bring up her child according to the old forms that her grandparents accepted; but let her bring it up in trust in the light and strength of its own inner knowledge. Let it feel the richness and power of its own soul and the enlightenment to be had from its own spiritual nature; and it will be able to go forth into the world strong and unafraid, compassionate and true. Such a one will be much better equipped to fulfil his highest destiny than one brought up with the limited idea of one earth-life and the fear of a punishing, revengeful God, and the conviction of his eternal sinfulness!

The doctrine of Reincarnation frees the mind of man. Suppose, for the sake of argument, I accept the belief in only one life, what have I to be proud of? What have I to revere? What have I to love? What have I to serve? Where is my God? What is life? Why, it is a farce or a horrible nightmare!

It is true that those old dogmas have

been accepted by very good and splendid people. But they were such in spite of those teachings, and their lives proved their essential divinity and bore out the teachings of Theosophy! One of the most beautiful of its doctrines is that there is eternal life for those who go out in the shadows as well as for those who go out in the light, because the divine laws are merciful.

Somewhere along the great journey we all have had a touch of the real spirit of Love — but only a touch; because if we had fully grasped all that the divine life has to offer us, we would not be here questioning; we would not have our present shadows and our heartaches.

Mothers and fathers know some of the depths of life and something of love. They can tell us the story. And they know that seventy years are all too short for their loved ones. We must have the opportunities of eternity in order to grow and to become and to evolve on the road of self-directed evolution. Such is the majestic teaching of Theosophy.

Accept it, and I assure you, you will walk in the light; you will touch the fringe of great truths; you will feel the majesty of the Divine Law, and the glory of living, the glory of loving, and the glory of serving, even in this one life. That is what Theosophy is trying to do: to liberate the minds of men, to bring them to a point of understanding, so that they can see these great truths from all angles and then begin to apply them to their own lives; to challenge themselves and bring themselves in the silence of their own inner chambers, in the quietude of their own hearts, to an understanding of the world's woes. When they reach that point, it will not be long before great changes will come.

But now the air is filled with the selfishness of human life. And how can we expect humanity to raise its standards and move out into the great, broad blue of an eternal Trust, if men have only seventy-seven or a hundred years in which to test themselves and to grow into spiritual maturity? I ask you.

SECTION IV

The Perfectibility of Man

"*The upward progress of the Soul is a series of awakenings.*"
— H. P. Blavatsky

THE PERFECTIBILITY OF MAN

I FEEL that my responsibility as a Theosophical teacher is very great, first on account of the necessity of adequately presenting our wonderful Theosophical teachings, and secondly because time is so precious; it is so valuable; and it is so very much misused even by intelligent and well-meaning people. One can appreciate time more in remembering that this particular moment will never be ours again. We must work and study.

The Preciousness of the Moment

In studying these great teachings, the heart is attuned to aspirations that lift one naturally out of the material and every-day way of thinking, into great hopes, great dreams, great visions, and great resolutions. While one may not respond always to such thoughts at the moment, still, sometimes from the smallest endeavor, if the conscience is clear and the motive high, great things can and do happen.

Not only is time misused, but human

life is also misused. The great majority of people today either have no serious beliefs at all regarding the soul and its destiny, or content themselves with a sort of half-belief in one earth-life only, without any knowledge at all of the future. The limitations that necessarily result from holding such restricted ideas greatly impede one's spiritual advancement.

But from the moment when one can attune his spiritual aspirations to a high standard of living, even in just one earth-life, the soul is immediately aroused and the results are beyond all reckoning; because each man is absolutely his own savior or his own destroyer. There is no question about this in the mind of any really thinking human being.

The treasures that belong to the inner life, that is to say, to the spiritual man, can be found only by research, by living in accord with the higher law of the spirit, and by holding firmly to aspiration. In following this path one will be better able to understand the Theosophical teachings and the wide field of thought that they embrace.

PROOF OF THE PERFECTIBILITY OF MAN 149

There are three outstanding principles of Theosophy which should never be forgotten; they are the doctrines of Karma, of Reincarnation, and of the actuality of human perfectibility.

Proof of the Perfectibility of Man

In regard to this last doctrine we have not only the belief, but the absolute knowledge, that man can attain through self-devised efforts to such a high degree of evolution that for any one period he may be said to have reached a state of relative perfection, but with the possibility of attaining a still larger and profounder state of development in future evolutionary periods.

When I first came into the Theosophical Movement I had only the Theosophical books and H. P. Blavatsky's knowledge of her Great Teachers on which to rely. But since that time, I have had in my own experience the proof of those truths which Theosophy expounds in reference to man's attainment of a state of perfection so far as it can be reached in one earth-life. This fact of relative human perfection was revealed to me through a personal meeting with such a man — one of our Great Teachers.

What I tell you is not the result of fancy, nor of dreams, nor of delusions, nor of an imagined self-sufficiency in my own spiritual discernment. I do not mean anything like that; but I do tell you what happened and what I saw and what I myself learned.

Not so many years ago, on my first tour through Egypt and India, I received an invitation to meet a Great Teacher.

I met this great character in India. Early in the morning before the sun was up I had a call from the Teacher's 'chela,' as they called him, who brought four servants and a special escort with their open palanquin. The chela acted as guide, and, with my maid, I went out up the mountains, and up the mountains, and up the mountains. The heat of the day was beyond anything that you can conceive of.

After miles of travel we arrived at noon at an almost unimaginable height. Everything except the great range looked small and insignificant. In looking out over the wonderful prospect, one could see how very easy it would be for one living up there all the time to have high aspirations and great ideas and to grow and to become royal and splendid. All that was possible.

I had my mind fashioned, as I think yours might have been, to see something quite remarkable — some astounding manifestation. But when I reached this person, he was standing leaning against a tree with an English jack-knife in his hand. He was cutting a little piece of wood. When he saw me he came to meet me, asking me to excuse him for a short time, because one of the bullocks with which one of his chelas was plowing had suffered an injury to his neck and he was trying to repair the yoke.

I looked straight at the man. Now, even in H. P. Blavatsky's time he was considered to be quite old in years; but he looked very young when I saw him. I would have said that he was then not more than thirty-two or thirty-three years of age. He appeared to be

Tibetan, dark of skin. His face was unlike any other that I had ever seen before. His whole life was lighted up with an inner light that had toned his features, had brightened his eyes, and had brought to him the glow of youthfulness and splendor of character. One could not look merely at his face. His whole figure commanded attention. Yet he was very unpretentious in manner.

I did not ask many questions, because I found that he anticipated them — questions that I had wanted an answer to ever since I came into the Theosophical Society; especially as to how I was to meet the heavy responsibilities that became mine when I was named as the Leader of the Society for life — the responsibility of helping to direct this Society of aspirants for spiritual wisdom and knowledge, at a time when I was unknown to all save perhaps one or two members of the Society.

I am trying to enter again into that meeting with the Teacher, so that I may give you whatever I am allowed to speak of.

In the first place, there was a conversation in reference to the little time that I could stay there. He urged me to hasten back in order to be inside the village before darkness, because there were bandits and queer people all about.

He then gave me many ideas, which of course might not interest the public, because they pertained very largely to my Theosophical work. Besides, it is very hard to find the language to describe the most glorious, superb, magnificent things in life. The most wonderful things that one ever sees in all their beauty can never be described.

But in his presence I felt the greatness of life, the true splendor of life, and its royal promise. My mind at this meeting was unusually alert and awake.

It was utterly impossible that this man was an impostor, as some might falsely think; because he referred to incidents in my own past that I had almost forgotten — incidents that at the time turned my footsteps in this or in that direction, and that finally led to my meeting with Mr. W. Q. Judge and eventually to his appointment of me as his successor in the leadership of the Society.

Mr. Judge had found me working among the poor of the slums — one might call them, — on the East Side of New York City, trying to help the unfortunate and to lift some of their burdens in an honest and determined way. That in itself was to me a great big world of effort. It seemed to me at the time that it was about as much as I could handle.

But here was a man who had grown great in unison with the higher expressions of life, to which he had attuned his whole being in utter self-forgetfulness. We all have this same opportunity; but he was a great soul, and welcomed this opportunity and profited by it daily.

We must all, sooner or later, believe in the marvelous powers of the spiritual soul of man. We must all sooner or later fathom the depths of our own nature and find therein the royal talisman of wisdom and truth.

This is what I found with him and in him.

The Illumination and Force of the Teacher's Presence

Just while I was standing there with him, I discovered anew, under the great force of his presence — and it came to me like an illumination,— that there was something indeed in me more than the mere mentality; that there was a vital, latent force inside me that desired to come out and inspire me to achieve things that I had never done before. It seemed to me as if I had never really lived before that moment, and never known so much about life as I then knew; and yet H. P. Blavatsky and Mr. Judge had both said that I was a Theosophist born. Yet this was the great day of my life — a day of greater promise for my work for all humanity.

Since then I have felt that it would be easy to go through fire and suffering and persecution and anything to push this message of Theosophy out to the world. The credit for this spirit of courage within me is not mine; it came to me from being in the presence of this Great Teacher, and from realizing in him to what heights a true man can reach.

There are some things which I cannot tell of this meeting, because they do not belong to the public, but only, possibly, to old and pledged members of our Society. But they were truly wonderful and grand. I will only add now that when I went to visit this Teacher, I was weighed down with the responsibility of carrying on the work of the Theosophical Society throughout the world and of meeting the conditions that I knew must be changed; because my Predecessor, William Quan Judge, had been ill for two years, and during his illness many things had drifted along in the Society by no means in accordance with the highest Theosophical standards.

But when I bade goodbye to that wonderful character and looked into his bright, kindly eyes (I never saw a pair like them), I had renewed life. I was then under the care of physicians, who declared I never would live to reach home. And traveling on the cars from town to town, it was daily expected that I would die. It may be very hard to believe it, but it should be believed; because I am truthful: I recovered my health, although I had been condemned by three of the best physicians in London and two in New York to die from Bright's disease.

No great magic was performed, and I did not become well the very next day. But physically and mentally I was so aroused that I steadily improved. My whole nature was alert, so that it was impossible for me to give way! And here I am still active, thirty years later! This really did happen.

I do not think it was any 'miracle.' I do not believe in anything supernatural at all. I believe that my soul was hungry; that I was to a degree weary of the weight of woe in the world. I saw people everywhere struggling, making their mistakes, and I was oppressed with the thought: "Poor me! What can I do to spread these great Theosophical teachings throughout the world?" Therein I was belittling my own power and almost losing sight of my own soul-strength, when I entertained such thoughts.

And then I met this Great Teacher. My soul-hunger was satisfied, my questions were answered, and my tired body responded and was cured!

Believing in Reincarnation, as we do,— that man has life after life in which to reach ever higher states of perfection,— one can imagine how much grander even this Great Teacher himself would be in yet another life!

The greatest language that was ever uttered can never fully bring to you the consciousness of your own essential divinity until you have aspired to even more than I speak of, until you have looked within yourselves, challenged yourselves, and rebuked yourselves just enough to find your strength to go forward and to become. Take Theosophy in this way and thus find its possibilities.

I absolutely challenge everyone, no matter what line of spiritual thought he has been following, to study the evidence that Theosophy presents in proof of its own intrinsic truth. You cannot get it elsewhere. You must have the basis, the anchorage, the footing, that Theosophy gives; and, above all, you must have a spiritual awakening. You cannot tell when it comes or how it comes, or anything of that sort.

The Challenge of Theosophy

All you have to do is to open your minds and look at the universe as something so vastly superior to anything you had dreamed of it as being before; look upon life as something sacred and grand and sublime in its promise and possibilities. Then recall what your aspirations and your dreams of noble action have been; think of your hopes and of the fragmentary touches that you have had of the spiritual life. Then you will find revelations upon revelations right within yourselves — in your inner nature. They are priceless.

I suppose that if we were told today that far off in the desert somewhere there were rich gold-mines waiting to be worked, we would all be up bright and early and start out in the morning and walk or run thither bare-footed, if there were no other way by which to reach the gold-mines! But if you are told of the beautiful spiritual treasures of Theosophical truth, that are right at hand in your own lives, in your own thoughts, within yourselves, few stir themselves even sufficiently to investigate!

Of course there may be some who are self-satisfied and think this is all nonsense and that you will not accept it. But a true Theosophist is fearless. That is one of the first evidences one sees of the glory and magnificence of these teachings of the Ancient Wisdom. These enable the true disciple to go through life unafraid.

Most beautiful of all, the true Theosophist is unafraid of death. He has a new view of death. And life itself is so lovely and sublime, if rightly lived, even in one incarnation!

No matter what your cares and your disappointments, you can depend on the inner life and find its peace without money and without price. When you realize this truth

THE CHALLENGE OF THEOSOPHY 161

and take it into your mind and your heart and into your very soul, you may be sure that life is joy, and that every moment is beautiful and sacred.

Each of you has a responsibility that you know very little about, unless you know something of Theosophy. You do not yet understand the real value of yourselves and your moments. So it is the duty of every man who can believe, and think, and dare, to fulfil his mission to the very end.

Theosophy tells you: Do not talk despondently about old age. Perhaps the body is indeed becoming old and tired; but think of the soul growing young in its splendid vitality, in its inner vision of things, in its realization of the value and the virtue of the spiritual life!

I know the day is coming, perhaps before I go to another life — certainly in the next twenty-five or fifty years,— when H. P. Blavatsky's sacred teachings, as they are imbodied in Theosophy, will be better understood and appreciated, even more than they are today, all over the world, and especially in Europe.

I say strange things sometimes, but I mean them; and I know what I am talking about when I tell you that Humanity will have to have many more shocks, more alarming tragedies and calamities, before the people awaken. Yet a true Theosophist must be able to look upon the most terrible things with open mind and stand unafraid throughout the storm. Why? Because Theosophy will enlighten the mind so that it understands, and the soul becomes receptive; it stands firm and is ready to meet and overcome all obstacles.

How trivial human existence is when viewed from the standpoint of only one lifetime on earth! Why, what can the man with even the greatest aspirations really do or work out in these few years that he passes here in this school of experience of one lifetime? But Theosophy says that he has another chance in another life, and after that other chances in other lives! Why, even Nature teaches us this lesson in its repeated seasons of going to sleep in its wintry rest and reawakening in the spring!

The Consciousness of the Soul-life

The one great need is for man so to arouse his mentality to the conception that he is a soul, that there can be the conquest by the soul. When men have reached this point, we shall not need any more prisons nor punishments. I do not believe we shall then have any more murderers anywhere; for the very atmosphere will be teeming with these finer forces that I am talking about, and which science is bringing forward to our view very rapidly. These will lead man to his heritage, to his light, to his own salvation.

Lest we should, perhaps when too late, look back over the record of our lives and be dismayed at the thought of what we might have done, I say again: Time is precious; Time is precious. In the short space of five or ten minutes, one can change his life for the better to an almost inconceivable degree.

I am not referring to matters beyond your comprehension. Let even those with the most obtuse minds, those who are indifferent to anything but to eat, sleep, and be merry, just feel once the thrill of the knowledge of the soul — of the real life! Awaken to that knowledge, and then time will become indeed very precious to you!

How royally and magnificently an awakened soul uses his moments! How joyfully he sets behind him all temptations and weaknesses! No vain regrets, nor great suffering, nor self-imposed martyrdom, nor anything of that sort! He just steps into the new life, rejuvenated, so to speak, renovated, restored to his spiritual rights and to that quality of knowledge that is essential for a man in order that he may understand his own responsibilities in life.

The reason why Theosophy is not accepted by everybody is that there are many people in the world, as everyone knows, who do not aspire. They have been miseducated for so long, as were their ancestors before them, that it is in their very blood to suppose that when a man dies, that is the end of everything; or, if he has been reasonably good, he goes to Heaven, and if he is not among the elect, he goes to the other place! O ye gods! What nonsense!

To the Theosophist, on the other hand, the picture is such that he learns to realize how precious life is. He values every moment of his time and makes good use of it. He applies his aspirations to real living. He stands constantly in the knowledge of his soul-life. He finds himself alert, alive, and moving positively onwards!

I hold that if one has the real teachings of Theosophy teeming in his very blood, he can never turn back. It is only those who merely half-place themselves in touch with these ideas and then play hide-and-go-seek with their own souls, who fail. — Yes, who fail for this life, but for whom there is another chance in the next life!

One who has the thrill of really divine aspirations sufficiently to believe himself a necessary factor in the spiritual scheme of human life, is always ready to look into Theosophy. Remember that Theosophy is nothing new; it is no innovation of recent centuries; it is very old, so old that we cannot go back to its beginnings, to those far distant ages when men and women lived closer to truth and to the simple life than they do now. It is as old as thinking man.

Real and Counterfeit Theosophy

I feel that it is my religious duty again and again to call the attention of the public to some of the popular delusions and false ideas that, unfortunately, many still have about Theosophy. I think it is abominable, outrageous, and a crime, that the word Theosophy, which means Divine Wisdom, has been so misused and misapplied by certain people who have sought to make themselves popular. This mistake does not happen among the members of our Society. In fact, I feel like saying that it would be dangerous if we ever gained such cheap popularity! There would then be too much likelihood of fraud, of imposition, and of the misrepresentation of great truths taking place. Such a condition is enough to stir the blood of every one of us.

We must all make our choice some time; and the question is, shall we do it now or shall we wait until another life? Then we shall look back and see the time we wasted and the opportunities we lost, and how we turned away from the true path.

These are the thoughts that come upon me so strongly in meeting people as I do when I lecture; because I know that they are very earnest; I know that they come to receive some light or some thoughts that will perhaps open up some new way for them — some happier way of thinking and living.

As I looked at our Memorial Temple of Peace on entering it today, dedicated as it is to the memory of my Predecessors, H. P. Blavatsky and William Quan Judge, I was thinking: "If this Temple had not been built, you would not be here today. And in my opinion you would have missed something that belongs to you, and which will ultimately greatly help you."

I am as sure as I live that there are always some who come to my lectures who will be affected with an honest interest in the sublime truths of Theosophy that can be found so easily. And that is what my work is. I call it my soul's energy, because I believe I am essentially a spiritual being, as all other humans are in essence. But I know that through my devotion to the principles of Theosophy, the Good Law has brought me here and has given me this opportunity to do what I can with an earnest heart to lift humanity's burdens. That is my true desire, for I love my fellow-men.

I am not a pessimist; for I realize that despite the crimes and the disappointments and the despair from which the world suffers today, there is a great promise of better things ahead. A change is coming. We are reaching the tether end of things as they are, and in the course of time something will happen that will suddenly arouse humanity to a realization that the only safe thing to hold to, will be the great and inspiring truths of the majestic Theosophical philosophy; for all that I tell you is verily your rightful human heritage.

SECTION V

The International Theosophical Headquarters

"Before we can achieve political reforms, we must achieve a reform in human nature."

— H. P. BLAVATSKY

THE INTERNATIONAL THEOSO-
PHICAL HEADQUARTERS

POINT LOMA, SAN DIEGO, CALIFORNIA

IT was nearly thirty-one years ago that the story of Point Loma as a spiritual and cultural center for the whole of humanity began.

On February 23, 1897, I laid here the corner-stone of 'The School for the Revival of the Lost Mysteries of Antiquity,' on what was then a barren, almost inaccessible promontory, practically uninhabited save by jack-rabbits, coyotes, and rattle-snakes, with no trees or houses, no water, gas, electricity, or other modern conveniences, and approachable only by trails scarcely worthy the name of roads, across the flats where now the U. S. Naval Training Station, the U. S. Marine Barracks, and the Ryan Air Field are located, which were frequently flooded by rain and high tides and rendered well-nigh impassable.

What a vast change these three decades have wrought!

To go back to my childhood-dream of the 'White City' that I would some day build in the 'Gold Land of the West': the travail of my own soul during the years that intervened before the realization of the dream seemed even remotely possible: the strengthening of my trust in the sacred laws of life, by General John C. Fremont, who told me in New York a few weeks before he died, when I described to him the place of my dreams, which I had never seen, that there was such a place in California, that he had seen it with his own eyes, and that it was at Point Loma, across the bay from San Diego: would doubtless be an interesting story to many, but it would lead me far afield from present purposes.

Suffice it to say that at the death of William Quan Judge, co-founder of the Theosophical Society in New York in 1875 with Helena Petrovna Blavatsky — the great Russian mystic of royal blood, cosmopolitan cul-

THE THEOSOPHICAL HEADQUARTERS 173

ture, and profoundest erudition — and her successor as the real Leader and Teacher of the Theosophical Movement in modern times, I found myself named by him in turn as his successor, with active centers all over the world whose members were enthusiastically devoted to the teachings of Theosophy — the Ancient Wisdom-Religion,— and within whose ranks at least a strong nucleus were eager to put into practice the teachings and to join me in establishing a World-Center for the exemplification of Theosophical principles in daily life.

The Headquarters of our Society were then at 144 Madison Avenue, New York. Shortly after Mr. Judge passed away there in 1896, I organized the first 'Theosophical Crusade' around the world for the spreading of the doctrines of genuine Theosophy, in contradistinction to the weird, fantastic, far-fetched, and often dangerous teachings that were then being promulgated and have with increasing persistence since been promulgated by certain so-called theosophists who shortened Mr. Judge's life by their cruel persecution of him and their opposition to real Theosophical principles.

Leaving New York on June 13, 1896, the party of American Theosophists, including besides myself some of the most earnest and prominent members of our Organization in this country, circled the globe and climaxed this tour by the laying of the corner-stone of our future work at Point Loma as already mentioned.

At that time San Diego had the appearance of a struggling mining town with little promise of ever being the beautiful city it now is nor the magnificent metropolis — the 'Port Orient' of the Southwest — which it is destined to become. But of course it had certain advantages which no one could rob it of — its fine landlocked harbor, its wonderful climate in the unsurpassed setting of purple mountains, calm seas, and blue skies the year around. And the best situation of all, in my judgment, was that which I chose for the World's Theosophical Center at Point

Loma. All that was required was the faith of far-seeing men in San Diego's future and the energy to make the vision an actuality.

And I must confess that, when at the end of our trip around the world, the members of my staff first visited Point Loma with me in 1897 over the rough country trails and under the conditions already described, their trust in their Leader was put to a severe test. It was hard to imagine that this 'jumping-off place' would some day be world-famous as a center of spiritual and intellectual culture and refinement, beautiful gardens, fine buildings of original architecture, magnificent homes and limitless possibilities.

Some of the hard-headed business-men of New York, who were members of my cabinet, said among themselves at that time: "Well, Katherine Tingley is all right as a Theosophical teacher, but petticoats cannot know anything about real estate, or she never would have had money invested in this God-forsaken spot." But there was no question of their devotion to Theosophy nor of their loyalty to the Leader whom it was their choice to follow.

And now, speaking solely from a material standpoint and leaving entirely out of consideration for the moment matters of far greater lasting importance to the world, I may mention that a portion of the land which was purchased by me in 1897 for $100 an acre I sold last year — still unimproved and not needed for my purposes — for $5500 an acre! Even an unimaginative real-estate dealer, who measures life in terms of profit and loss, can understand the force of these facts!

In February, 1900, I came with my staff of workers to Point Loma for permanent residence, and the International Theosophical Headquarters and all its departments were transferred from 144 Madison Avenue, New York. In May of that year I established the now world-famous Râja-Yoga System of Education at Point Loma.

What does Râja-Yoga mean and what are the principles upon which my school was established? I repeat here what I have said many times before in answer to similar questions:

'Râja-Yoga' is an ancient Sanskrit term; etymologically it means the 'Royal Union.' This term was selected by me as best expressing in its real meaning the purpose of my system of education, viz.: the balance of all the faculties, physical, mental, moral, and spiritual. The system was originated by me as the result of my own experience and knowledge, gained largely while working for the poor and unfortunate on the East Side of New York City.

I found that the conditions of suffering in the world were due largely to lack of knowledge governing human life. I realized that nearly all our systems of helpfulness were totally backhanded. We dealt then, and most people deal now, with effects rather than causes. After the damage is done we attempt to repair. I saw a picture of reaching down to fundamental causes, starting the child right and fitting him to meet the exigencies of life with some possibility of building his character, gaining self-confidence, keeping the upper hand, retaining originality, purity, and ideals, and leading a clean life. What I planned to do was to prevent the damage being done. The world was well equipped with havens for the beaten and the fallen. I wanted to evolve an institution to take humanity in hand before it was worsted in the struggle of life.

I said then, as I say now, that the truest and fairest thing of all as regards education is to attract the mind of the pupil to the fact that the immortal self is ever seeking to bring the whole being into a state of perfection. The real secret of the Râja-Yoga system is rather to evolve the child's character than to overtax the child's mind; it is to bring *out* rather than to bring *to* the faculties of the child. The grander part is from within.

In 1919 the Theosophical University at Point Loma, of which I have the honor to be the Foundress and President for life, was chartered by the State of California and has since been accredited by the U. S. Department of Labor as an institution of learning which may receive *bona fide* foreign students as non-quota immigrants.

What is Theosophy? Thus have I defined it in one of my first published works, *Theosophy: the Path of the Mystic:* Theosophy is no system of sterile thought but a light, a teacher, a companion, ever calling to compassionate action, ever urging to nobler efforts. Think of Theosophy not so much as a body of philosophic or other teaching, but as the highest law of conduct, which is the enacted expression of divine love or compassion.

My predecessor, William Quan Judge, in the opening paragraph of his work, *The Ocean of Theosophy*, thus defines it:

"Theosophy is that ocean of knowledge which spreads from shore to shore of the evolution of sentient beings; unfathomable in its deepest parts, it gives the greatest minds their fullest scope, yet, shallow enough at its shores, it will not overwhelm the understanding of a child."

And H. P. Blavatsky, Foundress of the modern Theosophical Movement, author of *The Secret Doctrine*, *Isis Unveiled*, *The Key to Theosophy*, etc., thus defines Theosophy or 'Divine Wisdom':

"Behold the Truth before you: a clean life, an open mind, a pure heart, an eager intellect, an unveiled spiritual perception, a brotherliness for one's co-disciple, a readiness to give and receive advice and instruction, a loyal sense of duty to the Teacher, a willing obedience to the behests of TRUTH, once we have placed our confidence in and believe that Teacher to be in possession of it; a courageous endurance of personal injustice, a brave declaration of principles, a valiant defense of those who are unjustly attacked, and a constant eye to the ideal of human progression and perfection which the Secret Science depicts — these are the golden stairs up the steps of which the learner may climb to the temple of Divine Wisdom."

A free correspondence- and information-bureau has been maintained for more than thirty years at the International Theosophical Headquarters, for the benefit of all who are seriously interested in Theosophy and the work here being carried on; and thousands of illustrated magazines, pamphlets, press-reports, etc., have been freely distributed to all quarters of the globe every year for the past three decades.

In conclusion, I repeat what I stated publicly about twenty-five years ago: that San Diego, which of course includes Point Loma, is destined to become the Athens of America. It is already an acknowledged World-Center.

[*The foregoing part of this section is an article written for and reprinted from the 59th Annual Edition of "The San Diego Union" of January 2, 1928*]

To the Resident-Members and Students at the World's Theosophical Center, Point Loma, California

The Spirit of Lomaland
THERE is enough of genuine spiritual virility in all of you to make this Movement tell for tremendous, mighty things in the next few years! Our Institution itself is impregnable, so long as we have the superb harmony, this royal unity of hearts and hands and minds, all working like one great golden stream of enlightenment down through the months and the years and the ages of the future. It is readily understood by those who open their minds to the truth that this Institution is the light of the world today; and every day it is throwing out more light, so that ultimately it will be the spiritual Mecca of the world!

So long as we join hands in this great mental and spiritual effort, just so long can we say in the truest and highest sense that we are marching on to victory — not alone to victory for ourselves but to victory for the whole world; for the whole world needs just the victory that we can bring, because never in the history that I know anything about, were conditions more terrible than they are today.

So we are constantly challenged, implored, and pleaded with from the inmost depths of our hearts and from the silent moments of our minds: "Do better! Grow stronger! Hold your heads up and live for the eternal verities!" These verities are to be found in the teachings of Theosophy. Live in Theosophy! Grow strong, pure, true, and beautiful; and all the rest will come to you!

This is a very sacred place to those who are closely connected with our Institution. The lives of very many noble men and women have been dedicated to it. It is no ordinary effort. Those who first came here to this uncultivated country came, in a sense, to a new land, far away from the advantages that most human beings deem essential. They came not with golden promises nor supported by the wealth of the world; but they came with one superb motive and a superb confidence, which, if we could ingrain them into the hearts of the mothers and fathers of today, would enable us to make the world over.

One might claim that all humanity has a certain quality of confidence; but the early Theosophical pioneers — particularly H. P. Blavatsky and William Quan Judge — had a rare confidence, a great understanding of life, and a broad and deep conception of all that human beings undertake to do.

The superb message that this one single woman brought — when she came to this country, unfamiliar with our language, unknown to our people, and facing the prejudice there was at that time against all innovations — her superb message has warmed the hearts of all the dear members and workers here and throughout the world, and it has influenced very many, far and near, to turn with greater hope to a brighter view of life.

The one great secret which she tried first of all to give to humanity was a knowledge of man's own essential divinity. And the next thing which we must all realize and take to heart and believe in, before we can understand ourselves, and before we shall be prepared to enter the next life, is the teaching of Reincarnation — of another chance, and another chance, and still another chance. Let us sing it out into the atmosphere in order to give a new hope to humanity! It is not a far-fetched doctrine; it is not a dream; it is a reality!

Our beautiful ideals, our hopes and our prayers and our yearnings, are not to remain forever unanswered! The future holds for us glory and beauty and charm and power and majesty; and, above all, Reincarnation brings home to all some conception of the inherent dignity of manhood and womanhood. These are the things we must think about.

The little children are teaching us the fundamental ideas, showing the joy of unity and co-operation and the gladness which they feel in loving the true and the beautiful. There is nothing to mar this happiness in

Lomaland. The dear mothers and fathers who have entrusted their children to us must feel that the little ones are breathing in the very essence of the things that all humanity should have.

We are not teaching the children Theosophy in any other way than by the example of the teachers' lives. And in the very atmosphere of co-operation among parents, children, and teachers, something is growing in the natures of these little folk that is preparing them for the next condition of life, when they are older.

I presume to take this opportunity to impress upon those who are not identified with our Organization that there is something to be found by coming into contact with the work of the Universal Brotherhood and Theosophical Society — especially with the members at our International Headquarters here at Point Loma, and most of all with the children. There is something in the very atmosphere of this Institution that all should have — especially those who are not satisfied.

Theosophy offers the key to the great problems of life: "Man, know thyself!" Through the study of the Ancient Wisdom, man can find the glorious anthem, the great symphony of life, that is ringing in the very atmosphere of our surroundings. But we have been too dead to hear. We must awaken and find the way and open the door and become the truest and grandest and the most superb guardians of the young ones.

It is our youth we must protect; and we can protect them if we will bring them closer to a realization of the meaning of life and its duties than we have before done. Then we shall make a great step forward in the advancement of the human race.

This is a very beautiful time, an exquisitely sacred and solemn hour. Our hearts have been touched. We have discovered something in the very depths of our natures, which perhaps we had never thought of before. It is a wonderful thing to meet together, especially in this World-Center, and to find ourselves rejoicing like little children.

I wish to congratulate mothers and fathers for showing the wisdom to send their children to the Râja-Yoga School. I believe that great blessings will come to them as a result of this — new life and new possibilities.

As for the little folk, they are making their lives very beautiful. Just as far as they do right, just as far as they are sincere, just as far as they love truth better than falsehood, just as far as they love the sunshine more than the shadows, just as far as they love their mothers and fathers and their comrades and all whom they know, they will find more in life than ever before.

Râja-Yoga is the sacred symphony of life that is ringing all about us. We have not yet heard it fully. But the sound is drawing nearer; the way is opening; and the light is breaking. The great spirit of love hovers over us, breathing out of the most tender parts of our hearts something beautiful which we cannot express. Let us try to make it something more for the whole world.

Let us make our lives more beautiful,

more true, and glorious examples; so that we will not only do our own parts, but encourage our little folk to a higher realization of life's possibilities.

If we can keep our hearts attuned to the true and the beautiful, even though we may be failing in a sense, and even though we have not reached the point that our aspirations demand, if we are moving forward, if we are up and doing, if we are striving to climb upwards, then we are safe, we are in the light and under the influence of the Higher Law, and we cannot go backwards.

So all of us are growing in spite of our imperfections. We are gaining the light and the strength that we need to grip the deeper problems of life through our own experiences. It is through these, I think, that we acquire the greatest knowledge.

I like to visualize H. P. Blavatsky and William Quan Judge as standing there in the doorway. I think each of them would say: "It is better than I could have expected." I believe they would have taken some long breaths and would have added: "But there is so much more that you can do. It is easily done, and right at hand, if you will only go directly for it, reach out for it, move away from your odd ideas and the 'unfinished business' in your natures. Move away from all the weaknesses you know of, and make a leap, so to speak! Take immediately the first one, then the second, and the third, and so forth."

Today marks another period in the progress of our work on the Screen of Time, which is a real thing to me. I think we have done well in many things since last year; and if I dare to look ahead three or four years I shall be smiling even more than I am today, and if I live, my eyes will be brighter, my heart will be stronger, my hopes will be greater. It all depends on you. This great work, this Theosophical Movement, depends on you even more than it does on the members throughout the world; for you are here at the Center, and you are closer to the realization of what the work means. You

THE SPIRIT OF LOMALAND

have not the distressing and destructive conditions of the world to meet every day.

It is a broad speech for me to make, but I make it: this body of people here on this Hill hold humanity in their hands. It is a tremendous responsibility; but oh! how splendid and glorious it is that we can be the great factors in this mighty work!

I do appreciate the work of every member here and throughout the world! Every department of our Organization tells a great story of the efforts and sacrifices that have been made by many, of the days and months and years of patient service! The unity of purpose back of it all haunts me. The charm of the whole beautiful spiritual work seems to breathe itself out into blossoming consciousness!

SECTION VI

The Theosophical Conception of Law and Order

> "*The difficulty, my friends, is not in avoiding death, but in avoiding unrighteousness; for that runs faster than death.*"
> — Socrates

THE THEOSOPHICAL CONCEPTION OF LAW AND ORDER

THE great truths of Theosophy are in themselves, intrinsically, so compelling, so convincing, and its principles are so powerful in arousing the virtues, that even a mere outline of it often proves itself actually a revelation, bringing to the consciousness of the listener unfamiliar with Theosophy something he never had before.

Theosophy the Enlightener

In the first place, Theosophy makes one better acquainted with himself. And while it makes one feel more keenly his highest needs, it also meets those needs. The most beautiful aspect of it is that it enables one to obtain in its teachings the remedy for the world's disappointments and heartaches, the explanation of the injustices of life, and the solution of all the serious problems of the time. And I declare that these problems cannot adequately be met in any other way than through the teachings of the Ancient Wisdom.

It requires no very great observation on the part of one who knows something of the menacing conditions of the world today to realize that somehow, somewhere, under some circumstances, in the course of humanity's evolutionary journey, important factors were overlooked.

In the first place, in the present age, the large majority of men do not dream of what their heritage is, or of what their possibilities are. Few indeed are happy, though some perhaps have the appearance of being so. Thousands and thousands live in the belief of the one life only.

I cannot conceive how the reasoning mind of man can contemplate the idea of the one life and be satisfied with it. If we consider merely his unfulfilled aspirations, the many things that happen that should not happen, and the much that his heart craves for that is not his, we must realize that he finds himself all awry unless he takes the broader conception of human life which Theosophy offers;

that is, that the doctrine of Reincarnation is true.

Then he looks out beyond the days and the years, beyond the one lifetime, and catches a glimpse of the infinite possibilities of the spiritual soul of man. He becomes imbued with the consciousness that he himself is essentially divine. From the time that he discovers this, all the aspects of life change. Where there was despair there is now hope; where there was darkness there is light; where there were errors there is truth.

Just these few words should be enough to startle the ordinary mind of man into looking at human life differently, into fashioning in thoughts, in aspirations, in dreams, in hopes, in plans, and in service, a quality of supreme manhood and womanhood that would outdo anything known at the present time, except to Theosophists.

Metaphysical research has its place, I am sure; but if we are to reach down to the absolute facts of life, we must have a basis of knowledge, and that knowledge must open

Theosophy Offers Truth

our minds to the truth, so that we are immediately convinced of the truth; so that we cannot escape it.

There is only one way of meeting the awful injustices that we know of, and that is by basing our knowledge on truth. Theosophy offers the truth.

How is it that the people of this century have drifted into the chaotic condition that now confronts us? How is it that the mothers and fathers of the present day, with all their longings, with all their love, all their devotion, all the yearnings of their hearts, and the disposition of self-sacrifice, have missed the key to that knowledge which is absolutely necessary in order to bring man to the consciousness of the divine life? That key is in man himself, in the divine side of his nature. When that is discovered it is the real enlightenment.

If we have no knowledge of the higher laws that govern our lives, and give us the hope and promise of another life, if we have no consciousness of our sacred duties — the duties of the real man, the soul — it is indeed wonderful that we can stand on our feet, as to some extent we do, and move along together without destroying each other. Why is this possible? It is because the divine ray is still present in every man and illumines his life as much as he permits it to do so.

The sun shines and gives you light; but it is very easy for you to turn your back on the light and live in darkness. So is it with these Theosophical teachings. We must meet them half way. We must meet the duties of life half way also. And in doing so, among other very essential qualities, we must cultivate an absolute devotion to law and order.

Even the best of men, those whose lives are unsullied, whose minds are full of good intentions and hopes, if they have not Theosophy are moving along in the shadows; they cannot find themselves; they do not realize the essential divinity of human life.

We must of course accept light from the inner life, from the inner portion of man's nature. We must move out beyond our prejudices and misconceptions and limitations. We must create a grand and magnificent picture of man's superb possibilities.

Watch Nature. See how the flowers grow, apparently without effort, in a natural way. One part works with another. There is inward harmony. Nature gives us wonderful examples and beautiful lessons; but we do not look at them. We are too much occupied with the bread-and-butter question. We have identified ourselves almost completely with the methods, the processes, and the non-essentials of the times, so that we have assumed artificial responsibilites.

Therefore it is very difficult for one like myself, or one more capable than I am, to bring that quality of knowledge to the mind of man that would convince him that without, and within, that afar, and near, are hidden forces and currents of the beautiful spiritual life. We must meet them in the natural way; work in harmony with them — with these higher laws that bring to us the superb consciousness of our own essential divinity. If we have this we have all, in a sense, that is needed; for the rest follows in natural sequence.

No Harsh Remedies

These treasures of truth are right at hand sleeping in the hearts of men. But they are ignored and set aside because the brain-mind depends upon many things with which it really has very little to do. The brain-mind has its place, of course; it gives us a certain quality of knowledge and enlightenment. But we must have a companion for the brain-mind — an accompanying power, and this comes from the spiritual side of man. The two must work in unity, the brain-mind enlightened by the spiritual, each fulfilling its proper mission.

Let us picture to ourselves the mothers of several generations back. Of course in some ways they knew more about the essential things of life than we do. But think what a progeny would have been theirs had they known of the deeper spiritual responsibilities of motherhood, had they drawn upon the rich inner knowledge that was sleeping within their very souls. Do you not believe that despite all that they taught, and despite all the obstacles that they overcame, they would have left a still nobler heritage to their offspring — that the spiritual part would have been cultivated at least equally with the physical?

With our overdoing in attention to the physical aspects of life and our lack of attention to man's spiritual life, the inner real life, we must admit that most of us are half asleep. If this condition had not existed for generations back, can you not believe that we would have less sin, less sorrow, less crime, and none of these monstrous murders that are such a dreadful social affliction today?

It is a sad picture — the present civilization! It is an appalling picture; it is a monstrous picture, that in this twentieth century we still believe it is our duty to attempt to correct human errors with force, with menacing punishments. It is proof of the lack of that spiritual knowledge which men should have in order to make them declare: "Withhold! No sacrifice of human life! No harsh and barbaric remedies at all!"

The spiritual nature of man, the enlightening and saving power within him, should come into action and cry out to indifferent people for more mercy, even for the most downtrodden, the most horrible and beastly creature in human shape. Mercy and justice! Can we remedy human error by force and fear? What examples do we set to our posterity when we attempt to do so?

How many people are there today who would have the courage to declare from the very depths of their hearts that they had found those qualities that make up the divine in man? Had they really found those qualities they could face the world with such knowledge and meet all opposition and prejudice, and even persecution and punishment. Not many; because we are a timid people; we have been educated to be timid; we have been brought up not to be sure of ourselves; we depend upon this book and on that book, on this teaching and on that teaching; we gather a little from each, and in the end there is more confusion and uncertainty than there was in the beginning.

The Hickman Case

But Theosophy offers the key to the ignorance of the age. That is why we preach and we work, so that we may help those who really need Theosophy. But the unfortunate psychology, not of this age alone but of the ages, has brought humanity to the point of despair.

There are splendid, noble fathers and mothers everywhere; but when their children arrive at the most crucial point in their development, the parents ask themselves, even if they ask no one else, for more light, for more understanding, for a better system of thought, for something that they have not yet found, so that their children may be protected.

Let us turn to this dreadful picture up in Los Angeles — that poor Hickman. We do not need to spend any moments in the horror of it all, the terror of it all. What we need to do is to give our thoughts to what remedies are to be applied. What are we promised in the future? How do you who have children know whether tomorrow one of your children may be taken from you in the same way?

Does the so-called remedy — the imprisonment and prosecution and punishment — save the others? Not at all. On the contrary, harshness engenders more crime; the psychology of crime increases, because there is not sufficient spiritual power existing today among the people to hold back the horrors of these things.

Going back to Hickman again: According to the best authority, I learn that Hickman was born less than ten months after his mother came out of an insane-asylum. There is something very serious to think about. People don't say much about it in the newspapers, but they keep reiterating and reiterating and reiterating the story of that awful crime, thereby actually cultivating hatred and the spirit of vengeance in the very blood of their children by associating them with such in their thought-life, thus creating added horrors!

Thought is a power. In one aspect of psychology, pure, high, and uplifting thought is a quality that we need in order to break down such conditions.

A law ought to be enacted to prevent the publication of such horrible crimes, so that our children may be protected from anything and everything that will soil their minds or interfere with their progress as souls.

In spite of our homes and our schools and our teachers, these things do happen; and it is a most awful travesty on justice and on manhood and womanhood that this is so. Everywhere there is confusion and conflict and chaos, and, let me say it in plain English, it is hell for the father and mother; it is hell for the man who is in the lowest depths of degradation; and it is a double hell for those who love the true and the beautiful and who realize their inability to overcome these conditions.

I read the statistics with great care. Every day they reveal to us the fact of a

THE HICKMAN CASE

large increase in the number of criminals. Stop and think for a moment that only fifteen or twenty years ago most of them were innocent little children in their mothers' arms. Yet all must see that something was lacking then for them.

At this point Theosophy offers its teachings of the duality of human nature — that man in his essence is divine, but that he is also imperfect. It is only through self-directed evolution that he can attempt to follow the path towards perfection. This all-important fact was never given to these children. Yet Jesus Christ taught it, and the ancient teachers taught it. But it was never fully impressed upon the minds of the people. So the struggling, heart-aching mothers and fathers, with their children and their problems, have never known the beauty and saving teachings of the spiritual law. And yet Theosophy can be obtained without money and without price.

May I tell you what I would do with Hickman today? I would make an example of him for the whole world. I would point out the barbarity of a law that would take the life of a human being, because legal murder is an outrage.

One might think differently of it if we could see better conditions resulting from it. If we could follow the soul of a man who had been hanged, through its evolution, we should find indeed that it has another chance after all; but we do not give it any chance here in earth-life.

If I had the control of Hickman's case, I should declare to the world that he is a mental invalid, insane beyond all power of description; because with his education and all that he had in his environment as a boy, if he had not had the seeds of insanity born in his very blood and nurtured in the ignorance of the age, he might have been giving as much happiness to his family as some of your children are doing. It is the law and order in which we bring up our children that determine whether their lives will tell for the salvation of humanity or its damnation.

Put aside your prejudice; look upon yourselves as greater than you have ever been before; believe that you have the power to discern, and see. "Judge not that ye be not judged." Let those words of Jesus Christ burn into your hearts, sink into your minds, and fire you with a sense of justice that will say: "Hands off! No repetition of this crime! No picturing of it in the newspapers! No brutal measures to force this insane boy to this or that and drive him still more insane!"

Believing as I do in the power of thought, let me tell you that we do not know how far this added insanity precipitated by the treatment that he has had, may affect disastrously many others of his kind.

One incident that may appear to some to be insignificant struck me as very significant. I noticed in the papers that in a cell either under or over Hickman's, a man committed suicide. My explanation of this would be that he was affected by the thought-atmosphere there. He was despondent; he had no faith in himself and that was enough.

He became psychologized by the whole affair and committed suicide.

And so it is that we are fashioning angels or devils as we go through life. I do not mean the kind of angels or devils described by the old theology; I mean man's own higher and lower nature: on the one hand his spiritual will, the angel; and on the other hand his weaknesses and passions and the undeveloped parts of his lower nature, the demons, which are very often the controlling powers in his life.

The more you cultivate the true and the beautiful and the more you accentuate the nobler side of your life, the higher are you climbing, the more are you overcoming and becoming.

Properly to express the divine laws, a human being must be well balanced. Balance is the result of law and order. Let parents give their children superb examples of such balance; so that the young minds shall be thrown neither to one extreme nor to another, but grow through natural evolution under the guidance of those who care for them.

I hold that a child from the time it is born until it is seven years of age is at the mercy of either the good or the bad, the strong and the weak. It is at the mercy of its environment. If it is guided rightly from its earliest stages of growth, when it reaches the age of seven years something happens to it, like a spiritual baptism. It is like the blossoming of a flower. Its growth has been going on all the time. But by the proper nursing and through evolution it reaches a point where it develops into an exquisite blossom. Beautiful Nature is our teacher.

I wish that I could leave out the sound of my voice from any Theosophical teachings, because the moment such teachings come through the lips of any one, their beauty and grandeur and truth are limited. Each one, too, must find them for himself. A man may be thirsting for a glass of water; he may be told where there is water; but until he drinks the water for himself he cannot quench his thirst.

There are law and order in the great universal Scheme of Life. It is law and order that keep the stars in their places, and keep the sun shining as it does, within bounds, so that it benefits us and does not destroy us. It is a spiritual law; it cannot be moved; it is immutable. So must we live in seeking to find spiritual advancement. We must keep in mind the influence of law and order as we seek knowledge.

What should we do to a poor soul like Hickman? I can fancy that if he were my charge I would have him carried far off, up into the mountains to a hospital, surrounded by great beautiful trees, with an abundance of sweet, pure air. I would give him something that nobody had ever thought of giving him before.

We cannot undo the wrong that he has done. The sacred Law of life will work that out with him; but you could set a splendid example of mercy; so that even those so far degraded as almost to have lost their manhood would respond to the example of your orderly life, of your mercy and generosity, and love of justice. New light and added forces of spiritual being would spring into life, and awaken men and women to their real duty and to the spirit of brotherly love towards all their fellows.

SECTION VII

The Drama

I learned to love Shakespeare when I was a little girl, and I have been faithful in my loyalty to him all these years, reading and re-reading his plays, and thinking over his life and his creations, and admiring the soul of the man, who, under such difficulties, pulled himself through and made himself a world-star of the first magnitude in the intellectual life of humanity.

THE DRAMA

THE DRAMA has been very much on my mind within the last two or three weeks, because we are preparing for a presentation of one of the ancient mystery-dramas of Aeschylus at the Greek Theater here. Moreover, this seems to me a most opportune time for one who loves the true drama to accentuate the fact that the real drama was taught and presented in a magnificent way centuries before the birth of Christ.

"The Eumenides"
April, 1927

If one looks into ancient history, especially into that of Greece, one finds much that is both interesting and inspiring in connexion with the religious aspect of the drama. There was a time when the Greeks, as many as thirty thousand of them, would meet in the morning and carry out their devotion to the superb religious dramas of their master-poets until sundown!

Thinking of this fact, one can realize

how much we have lost through the intervening years. It is only occasionally that one hears anything about the classical Greek dramas today. Of course, scholars are familiar with them to a degree; but the average person today, even among those who think, knows little about antiquity; and it is a great pity that the bread-and-butter question should be of such absorbing concern that much of the beauty, and grandeur, and inspiration, and splendid spiritual support to be derived from the ancient dramas, are lost.

One of the objects of the work which I represent is to create a greater love for the higher qualities of the drama, and to impress again upon the human mind through the drama, the necessity for a religious view of life. To the ancients the drama was not merely a means of relaxation and amusement: it was a part of their religious life. And it is well known what lovers of the good, the true, and the beautiful, the Greeks were. Those familiar with their literature know what great ideas and sentiments they have left to us.

I consider the drama one of the most essential factors in the education of our people — especially in the education of the youth. Let them become familiar with the splendid dramas and philosophies of antiquity, instead of allowing them to fill their minds with the trash that we meet nowadays in the efforts of many theatrical producers, which, far from raising the minds of the youth to a higher contemplation of life — to some conception of the truth and of the magnificent aspects and possibilities of man — drag them down, or at best merely entertain, or please the fancy, and amuse.

There is a sanctification that comes from studying and working over one of these ancient dramas. I know that after each performance of *The Eumenides* here in our Greek Theater it takes me several days to come back to the every-day way of living. So one can imagine with what joy our members here at the International Theosophical Headquarters, who have come from many parts of the world, joined with me in my work of raising the drama to a higher level by a revival of the classics. There is no money in it, no pecuniary recompense, no honors, no fame, for any who take part in it. But there is an inner joy that no language can express.

The study of Theosophy, particularly as applied to the study of the ancient dramas, gives us many splendid secrets — secrets which I fancy if one had to pay for them, he would go to the ends of the earth to find! But Theosophy gives them freely, as far as one wishes to understand and accept them.

Real drama affords man one of the grandest opportunities to understand himself. I refer particularly to the ancient Greek dramas. Practically every line in *The Eumenides*, for instance, contains a profound truth of the ancient Mysteries. The more one reads, the more one desires to know about it. The more he studies, the more enlightened he becomes. Here he sees clearly that man, being dual in nature, possesses on the one hand the attributes of the spiritual soul and the possibilities of great perfection; while, on the other hand, he has much in his nature that, unless he conquers it, will destroy him.

We must move into the feeling of the sacred drama — the trend of men's minds in their aspirations, in their devotion, in their love of the true and the beautiful. Even those who make the greatest mistakes and who are most indifferent to the real drama of life, are religious in the deepest side of their nature. They are a part of the great human family, divine in origin. Nothing is lost. None can be overlooked.

We should look upon human life as a great drama — a great mystery-drama, filled with limitless possibilities. The kingdom of heaven is within; and so is the kingdom of hell, which is the kingdom of ignorance, of dissatisfaction, of delusion, and of unhappiness.

If we wish to help to purify the world, to purify our nation, our city, and to breathe the sweet air of a new life, we must first allow ourselves to dream of the possibility of it. We must dare to go towards it and become the masters and understanders of our own lives first of all. Then we shall have the key to understanding the real drama of life.

SECTION VIII

𝔗𝔥𝔢 𝔑𝔢𝔴 𝔇𝔞𝔶
𝔈𝔞𝔰𝔱𝔢𝔯, 1928

"For nothing else but the body and its desires causes wars, seditions and fightings."

— PLATO

THE NEW DAY—EASTER, 1928

THIS is Easter-day! How very wonderful it would be if all humanity could every day in the year find their Easter — in themselves, in their souls, in their friends, in Nature, in the Divine! What a wonderful world we should have! And if it is possible to do this today, it is possible ever afterwards!

Easter

The divine light that is ever attempting to shine in the hearts of men is an ever-present, divine power. But poor humanity has drifted so far away from its moorings, from the realization of its own essential divinity and its royal heritage, that it has lost its way; yet not lost it entirely, as is proved by the fact that at every Easter we do find ourselves meeting together — many of us strangers — touched more deeply, perhaps, than at other times, with the outward manifestation of gladsome Nature, which we to our loss so little understand.

The Easter-celebration is very ancient in its origin. For thousands of ages before Jesus Christ, people absolutely believed in their own essential divinity; not just an individual here and there, but the great sweeping mass of the people in those olden times had a firm belief in the essential divinity of man's soul. They were aware of the beautiful possibilities of following the divine urge in us: while we have been drifting steadily downwards.

No matter how much wealth, or intellect, or education, or culture we have in the outward sense, what man really needs to give him the secret of living, the 'worthwhileness' of life, so to speak, is that quality of the soul and of the heart which bespeaks the divinity within. Each one of you has known it at some time and under some circumstances; otherwise you could not smile; you could not love anything; you would be at cross-purposes with everything. It is the eternal, divine life growing in the hearts of men.

Nature awaits all the time our recognition of the wonderful, invisible forces of the inner life. And the reason we do not take into our souls the sweeping forces of these divine, eternal, permanent qualities, is that we have lost faith in ourselves, in our fellowmen, and in our inner God.

That is the great trouble with humanity. If it were not so, we would have no war, no semblance of war. We would all be living together peacefully, doing the duties of everyday life, but spiritually conscious of the inner life, drinking in the strength and the beauty of the eternal life.

It is only those who have felt the touch of the Divine who can talk about it; and those who have felt it more than once can talk about it perhaps better than those who seem not to know anything about it. But the fact is that every man, when he tests his strength, when he challenges his own soul, reaches out into the sunshine of life and finds that life is worth living.

In the ancient days, ages before the time of Jesus Christ, the Pagans understood the symbology of the Easter-time; and simply because in later days they introduced many things that were not right, the Pagans have been much looked down upon. But the celebration of Easter was originally a Pagan festival, which the church-fathers later adopted and turned into a Christian observance when they found that the ideas associated with it were so ingrained into the very lives of the multitude that it was of no use to attempt to change them. That is the real history of the origin of Easter.

Theosophy is the Ancient Wisdom and it gives its students wonderful lessons in interpreting the symbology of ancient beliefs and customs. The teachings of Theosophy emphasize the importance of the inner life and the spiritual side of man, which is eternal.

To the true Theosophist death is very beautiful; for in death the spiritual soul, the inner life of man, finds its place — it is resurrected. The body is tired and worn out, but the change for the next life is advancement, progress, for those who wish it; and those who turn away from it will have to wait for their next turn, their next incarnation.

When I look at the beauties of Nature, the flowers and the trees give me more sermons in every breath I draw than have ever been preached or printed. We can find our own souls in the silence of Nature; and also in the innocence of little children.

The real purpose of the ancient Easter-festival of the Pagans was to impress upon the minds of men the power of the Christos or Christ-spirit that is in every man.

If there is any place in the world where man can find his own soul, I think it is in California. The flowers and the trees, the mighty ocean and the breezes from the mountains and the sea, and the caressing climate, are forever whispering to us the secret of the real meaning of Easter.

Theosophy gives us a closer knowledge of man's needs and possibilities, and consequently there grows in our hearts a royal sympathy for all humanity; and sympathy is the very thing that the world most needs today. So think of the force that must be at work on inner lines, on a day like this, in the aggregation of thoughts and lofty feelings experienced by millions all over the world in their Easter-celebrations.

If I could convince you of the beauty and the grandeur of human life, and the possibilities of man's soul-advancement through self-directed evolution, it would be worth more to you than all the wealth of the world; it would be something that could not be taken from you. It would give you such a divine trust in humanity that you could not rest without working for something better for all mankind. Self-directed evolution means the salvation of man.

We have opportunities continuously of making every day an Easter-festival, a day of the resurrection or the evoking of the spiritual side of our natures; for every man is a Christ in degree. But we and our ancestors before us have been moving along under the psychology of the ages, half-blinded with the teaching that Jesus alone was the special son of God, and that the rest of humanity were miserable sinners whose only salvation lay in something outside themselves. Such a conception deprives humanity of its rightful spiritual heritage.

But on a day like this, when millions are celebrating the Easter-festival all over the world, people are very much affected by the idea of the resurrection, even though they do not fully understand its meaning. For the time being it takes one away from the limitations of worldly things, away from the distractions and allurements that blind so many, away from one's peculiarities, his idiosyncrasies, his fears, his doubts, his mistakes, and the pains of everyday existence. These all disappear when one can view life from a Theosophical standpoint, and realize that the meaning of the resurrection is the coming of the spiritual soul in man into its own splendor.

We are all travelers along life's pathway, aiming to reach perfection. Theosophists believe in the doctrine of Reincarnation, and declare that it is the great process by which it is possible for man to advance towards this goal of perfection. Keeping these thoughts in mind, and invoking the power of the higher imagination, we can all create ideals in our own lives, and then work for them, strive for them, and realize them in degree.

A recognition of man's essential divinity is the spiritual basis on which to stand. Let this be well fixed in the mind. Clear away the rubbish that is there, and begin to believe in man's royal spiritual heritage.

Let us leave humanity out of the picture of this world of ours for the moment, and consider the grandeur of Nature. Let us think of the flowers as we have never thought of them before. They preach eternity to us; they also preach Reincarnation; they tell us in their silent language that man is divine in essence; and in that one keynote, the whole great program of man's future advancement is held.

On a day like this, it is impossible to look upon Nature in our usual every-day way.

The flowers talk to us; the great ocean, the sky, the majestic trees that cover the land; everything away from man himself preaches the splendor of Eternal Life.

Theosophy and Christianity

Easter is a day of invocation not only to Nature and the gods but to every human being, to awaken, to arouse himself from half-sleeping, half-thinking, and to step out into a new world of beauty and great possibilities, bringing the divine man to the conscious recognition of the masses.

It is a fact that humanity has been moving along half-asleep ever since the time when Christianity was established. In saying this it should be remembered that true Theosophists find much in Christianity that is very beautiful, and much of this was found also in the Pagan religions; but many of the forms are not accepted. The forms of the Christian religion were fashioned by the minds of men. Let us not question their motives; let us assume that they did it for the benefit of humanity. But a religion that constantly reminds one of his sins, of his mistakes, and of his weaknesses, appeals principally to the negative side of man's nature, especially when the effort is forever repeated to have him realize that the only way by which he can be 'redeemed' is by resting all hope of spiritual advancement upon faith alone or on a power outside himself.

Let it be remembered that true Theosophists are never disposed to belittle Jesus. We look upon him as a great Initiate; we bow to the divinity of his nature; we have learned that he was one of the few great men who, at different epochs, have arisen to a position where they have consciously known their essential divinity and have lived in it and have rejoiced in it, smiling with complete trust in it.

Jesus loved humanity; he served it gloriously and magnificently; and the picture comes to me that the saving power of the divine that was in him is in all of us, if we could only reach it, if we could only be aroused and awakened, as Jesus was, if we would look forward and accept the spiritual heritage that belongs to all humanity.

With this conception, and with a conviction of the truth of the sacred doctrine of Reincarnation, which gives man opportunity after opportunity in his different lives, at the various stages of his progress, we can face the inmost weaknesses of our own natures with the bright picture ever before us of the godlike qualities lying hid in man. But these must be aroused, developed, accentuated, if man is to advance in self-directed evolution.

Man cannot face the universe with that quality of trust that is the working of the spark of divinity within him, until he is generous enough to see that some of this same spiritual life is in all humanity.

This is the meaning of the New Day: It is the opportunity for man to challenge himself, to look within himself for the divine ray that is his real Self. It is a superb day for making new resolutions and holding to them. No matter what the difficulties are, no matter what the sorrows are, no matter how poor and forgotten and ignored and apparently helpless one may be, Theosophy teaches that this is the right of every man.

But each must find the path for himself; each must seek the way of salvation through his own efforts rather than to wear his soul out, weighed down with the consciousness of his weaknesses and of his mistakes, depending upon everything but the godlike qualities within himself. Bear in mind, this negative attitude of thought leads a man away from his rightful spiritual heritage. No wonder, then, that he ceases effort and follows the downward path of degeneration, along with those who lack the spiritual knowledge that should be theirs!

The man who believes not in his own essential divinity, who has in his thought no future beyond the one life on earth, is verily to be pitied; for truly he has lost his way. But Theosophy says that not even he is permanently lost; for there is another chance for him too. So no matter from what standpoint or premises one may argue, he will find that Theosophy is the panacea for all the ills of the world. However disturbing the psychology of the age, it cannot affect the real deeper divinity of man, which the spiritually awakened man alone has the sacred privilege of understanding.

What Theosophists are trying to do is to arouse humanity as a whole; to awaken it, so that it may not waste so much time in despair, so many incarnations in its long turns and twists off the path, while living without the knowledge of Theosophy.

Today, *now*, this very moment, is an appropriate time for man to invoke something new and better within himself. He cannot help others until he believes in himself — note this, please. He must know the inner quality of his divine nature; he must feel its presence constantly — its support, its inspiration. Verily, he must feel that inner urge which accentuates the fact that all men are immortal; that inner urge which makes humanity like unto a host of young gods traveling along the path to perfection.

Why waste your time in fears and doubts

or in discouragement and despair? Learn to respect the holy part of man's nature — the divine soul,— that each life may be pure and true and strong and clean and forceful. Above all things, realize the sacredness of human life. This is what every awakened man and woman must do. And it is the easier way; it is the way that will keep the sun shining in one's heart and eyes, even when he is parting from his tired and worn-out body.

Can you not go with me in thought for a moment to a sick-room, where the immortal soul of someone is winging its way to the Eternal, while the body is breathing its last on this plane? Can you not see what a marvelous difference the knowledge of Theosophy makes? How differently one meets death, who believes in his own essential divinity, who knows his spiritual rights, who has moved along the path of self-directed evolution: how different such a one meets death, I say, from the one who accepts merely on faith the philosophy of redemption through another!

Consider the glorious picture of a man

in his godlike qualities, convinced of the truth of Reincarnation, going forward along the path fully alive, pregnant with bright hope and divine trust, believing in this life and another and still another, and meeting eternity with the courage of a god! With this consciousness pulsating in his very blood, he would set his difficulties behind him and become a glorious and splendid example of the Christ-spirit!

If we could step forth into the silence of Nature with new courage, new trust, new hope, seeking within ourselves the eternity of things, it would not be long before the very trees and the flowers would talk to us, and the swish of the ocean washing the shores would sing a new song to us, and the sun would shine more gloriously: the very silence of Nature would preach to us the greatness of the Christos-spirit in man; of man living in his dignity, in the consciousness of his power, making every moment so sacred and sweet and clean as to wipe out the record of past mistakes and prejudices and hatreds and dislikes; bathing in the light of man's godlike nature, feeling the whole universe alive with the possibilities ahead for the world's children — for you and for me!

Would not this word-picture be excellent for some of the poor criminals in prison? What do you think about the wretched fellows that are soon to be hanged? True, they have done great wrong. But now those who call themselves the helpers and protectors of civilization are daily repeating in cold blood, under the sanction of man-made laws, the very crime of those incarcerated! What hope of redemption and reformation does such barbarous work afford? Under what conditions does the soul, the immortal part of a prisoner condemned to legalized murder, leave the body? What prospect is there of his doing any better either in this life or the next, when he goes out filled with the memory of man's vindictive punishment?

Just as long as we permit this relic of the dark ages to continue, just so long are we contributing to the brutalizing of humanity.

Just so long as we make such mistakes, just so long as we follow false teachings, just so long as we ignore the great and beautiful truth of man's innate divinity, just so long are we making bad karma for our country and for all countries, as well as for ourselves, and just so long are we helping the great human family on the downward path of retrogression.

But instead of this, why not set ourselves to do right in the thought that on this glorious new day of the resurrection, we should prepare ourselves for the battle of life: which will mean victory and permanence for all those things which go towards the enlightenment and uplifting of the human race?

All through history we read the wonderful records of great and splendid characters. Some were materialists; others belonged to this or to that faith; and many of them did soulful things to lighten the burdens of the world. But think what they might have done, if they had had the inspiring knowledge of Theosophy!

Consider, for example, some of our great musical geniuses. Surely they must have been in preparation in former lives for their marvelous work in this life! Think of them making their records of glorious victories along the path; and then think how much more glorious their victories might have been, if they had had at all times the consciousness which they must have had at the times of their inspiration, when they were touched by the enlightening and uplifting power of the true and the beautiful! They must have had it at such times; but the great thing is to be sure of it at all times, to hold within oneself the consciousness of the essential divinity of man to such a degree that nothing can uproot its power. This is one of the greatest treasures and most blessed privileges that anyone can have.

When one reaches this point, he will not have to talk so much in order to make people understand even a little. His very soul will be illuminated and his voice will speak in tones that he has never made before. His very presence will sing to the world in the silence of the glories of the Higher Law, of the eternal man, of the peace of the world, and of love for all humanity.

Knowledge of Theosophy Essential

Then, if one allows his imagination to spread out a little farther, he will vision the marvelous triumphs that mankind will achieve even in one life. But of course it takes time — everything worth while requires time to consummate.

Many good people suffer today unnecessarily, because they do not understand Theosophy, or the meaning of life's apparent injustices. So they become discouraged and lose faith in themselves and then they lose faith in humanity.

So it is time that we talked of the New Day. It is time that we brought again to the attention of the world the great philosophy of the Ancient Wisdom, that humanity may know what it holds for them. It is time that we ingrained into our minds, into the very basic forces of our natures, the truths of Theosophy; for Theosophy is really the panacea for all the ills of the world.

Then life would be beautiful; our minds would be in accord with all that lives; our souls would be enlightened on the journey along the eternal path; our vista would be enlarged; every truth would have a mighty meaning.

Set aside arguments; rise above mere reason; reach the spiritual conception, which is the rightful heritage of every man, as he advances along the road of self-respect and self-control and enlightenment.

The very best remedy today for most of the ills that humanity suffers from is the practice of self-control. But how can we expect human beings to practise self-control without the key that unlocks the secrets of acquiring self-control? This key is the knowledge of man's essential divinity. This is the key that opes the door to many of the mysteries of life and explains them. It makes a golden road for man to tread along the journey of his life. Conscious of his essential divinity, of his spiritual dignity, of his sacred responsibilities, man may walk verily like a god.

There are, of course, different degrees of godhood — I am referring to the godlike qualities in man; for there is innate divinity in man and he will find it after a while, after many experiences on earth, after many trials and failures in different lives.

Theosophy is ever aiming to teach humanity that life can be made very beautiful in spite of the fact that it is so often made the other way.

But what an insult to the great Central Source of Light for anyone to accept the idea that the Creator established this earth to be filled with millions of human beings, who have seemingly nothing to do with their coming into existence, who have no choice in the matter, and that then this same Creator allowed his own creatures to be born in sin and condemned them to go through life powerless to meet their difficulties and to overcome their weaknesses! What a horrible thing to think of! What chance has humanity, if such a doctrine be true?

The New Day Today is the New Day! It is the beginning of a New Time! In times to come we shall hear of this as the greatest day we have had for long, long years. Something is going to happen that will reveal this in such a way that many will turn towards the light. Verily it is a glorious day, a day of peace — perfect in degree. The air about us now is full of joy. The very flowers talk to us! Nature is pleading with us, singing the song of the soul-life of man. But the message of this New Day is the message of reform in the highest sense — the knowledge of the Universal Life ever in us and with us and working ever for us: and of our essential divinity to believe in, to live in, and to become.

SECTION IX

Universal Brotherhood

"Karma does not always manifest itself as suffering, by any means: it is quite as likely to produce joy as sorrow."

— W. Q. JUDGE

UNIVERSAL BROTHERHOOD

Salutations to All the People of the World

OUT beyond all the many manifestations of inconsistency in human life, and the cruelties of man to man, those who have a trust in their own essential divinity and that of their fellow-men have yet a royal hope that a New Order of Ages will come ere long to the restless people of the world. Without this hope life would not be worth living.

So at this Christmas-Time, with our hearts burning with the desire to lift Humanity's burdens, we bid the Season's Good Cheer to all the people of the World.

May this Sacred Holiday-Time bring a new promise of better things! And may we enter the New Year with a courage born of our divine trust in the justice of the Higher Law!

Salutations! Salutations!

December, 1927.

A NEW-YEAR'S MESSAGE

TO THE RESIDENT-MEMBERS AND STUDENTS AT THE WORLD'S THEOSOPHICAL CENTER, POINT LOMA, CALIFORNIA

WE need all the fine touches of the beauty and pathos of the heart, before we can arrive at a conception of what our duty is.

We have been psychologized by the world, so to speak, from the day we were born. That psychology goes far back. Much of it is in our very blood. The battles and struggles that we have in life over things that to most of us seem so serious and so hard, are put upon us by our own limitations, especially by our limited conception of only one earth-life. The Theosophical teachings concerning the hereafter reveal to us the glory of eternity. But the hindrances of the past hold man down, shut out the light from him, so that in very truth often he loses his way.

The heart-touch evoked by the children brings a benediction to all. We can feel great promise for the future even in the midst of the pleasure of the moment, the joy of the occasion, and all the glorious evidences of the heart-touch everywhere felt. We can do greater things; we can have a deeper and more profound conception of life; and we can step out into a new world of thought that will be all of our own creation.

Perhaps more than at any other time in our lives we are knocking at the portals of a new epoch. The higher our resolves the more will those outside be helped. There is no limit to the power of a beautiful thought. The force of many beautiful thoughts and splendid resolutions combined must bring about something that we have never had before.

So I say from the depths of my heart: A Happy New Year! Many, many happy New Years!

Surely the time is coming when we shall have a new view of the grandeur and beauty of life, in spite of all the horrors that we see in the world around us. A new energy has been born, which stands out in the potency of spiritual power by contrast with the degrading and horrifying experiences that the world is going through.

My heart is touched with a deeper quality of compassion than I have ever felt before, for all those who have erred.

The time will come when all will find what the inner life means — the beauty of it, the glory of a soul filled with aspirations towards a perfect life, a pure life, a noble life, a trusting life, born into an atmosphere where each can go through the struggles unafraid! There is nothing for us to be afraid of except our own weaknesses!

Something new and splendid will surely spring from our thoughts, because the Higher Law brought us together. Let us knock at the doors of our own hearts, realize the spiritual dignity of human life, and dare to step forward and demand from ourselves the restoration of that knowledge and that inner satis-

faction which the heart craves. Then we
shall find the joy of living.

Remember that the outer life is the
transitory and the inner life is the eternal.

Thousands of people all over the world
look upon New Year's Day as a time in which
to make new resolutions. The beginning of
new efforts awakens in the minds of those
who are looking away from their restlessness,
royal hopes and aspirations. It creates new
ideals and arouses new hope.

Among the representatives of different
religious beliefs, each religion is supposed to
be the superior one to those who participate
in it. Yet we all know that there are no end
of errors in many of the teachings of the
various religions.

The first thing to wish for and to hope
for is that all humanity were united in the
living spirit of Universal Brotherhood. Their
comprehension and their ideals have far outgrown the old ideas.

An entirely new act, in a sense, has been
created in the great drama of life for Theo-

The Living Spirit of Universal Brotherhood

sophists; because it is impossible for us to accept the idea of a personal God. One who accepts that idea is looking back upon himself, with a very limited view of the future, if any at all.

Many men at present are shut in, held down, and blinded by the thought of *only one life on earth for man*. Fancy! Only one life of a hundred or a hundred and twenty years at the most for an aspiring soul! It is very pitiful that any religion should hold man down to a belief in only one life.

I have often met those who were nearing death; and many who had been most certain of their future in heaven and of the love and mercy of their God when in health, were later full of questionings, and many of them passed out of this physical life in black doubt.

But if man looks forward to the future at all seriously, he is conscious of something intangible that the soul senses, that the heart craves for, and that the mind conceives, but that has not yet been reached. Outside the ranks of Theosophists many humans approach the next life with fear and doubt.

More than anything else the world needs today a new quality of Optimism. One need only see the statistics of crimes committed and the menacing conditions that result therefrom to realize that humanity is today on the downward path. Of course, many may be aspiring in their intentions to raise themselves, but present conditions are a bad omen for the future. The fact is that man is retrograding at the present time through his own wilfulness.

We have our mind with which we think. That is what the mind is for. It is a great factor in man's evolution. But it is not the saving power for him. He must clarify the mind to such a degree that, while thinking rationally, he will turn away from extreme ideas, and from imagining that his own notions and opinions and idiosyncracies are superior to anything else in life. The moment one imagines that, he is in serious danger.

What is needed is that we should throw ourselves sufficiently and with courage into our inner natures where we shall find true answers to our questions. Then we shall be assured of finding ourselves on the right path.

Surely it does not require a word from me to show that humanity as a whole is not at present on the right path. If all humanity had Theosophy as an inspiring guide, they would also have an optimism that would lift man above his weaknesses, make him forget his lack of faith in himself and his fellows, and, as a result, the world would present a very different picture from what it does today.

After a very short while man would begin to find himself, to find that real life is beautiful and joyful; that the disagreeable experiences which all must go through, afford the necessary lessons which we must learn. We cannot pass these by. If we overlook them we shall have to take them up again later, either in this life or in some future incarnation.

On this beautiful New Year's Day, let us have a clear view of the essential dignity of humanity, of the spiritual life of man, and of the eternity of the divine spark within us.

Then we shall realize that the secrets of life all lie within, and that man must be their revealer to himself. Then we shall make royal New Year's resolutions — not resolutions that come merely from the brain-mind or from foolish sentiment, but resolutions born absolutely from man's spiritual will, which is above ordinary mental processes.

Man's spiritual will is the faculty that enables him to round out his life nobly, to build up his character, to enlarge his mentality, so that his whole being works in harmony with those higher laws which hold us all safe within their keeping.

The awful crimes that are such a menace to the future of our country are leaving terribly black marks on our national history. There is no country in the world that has such a record of crime as America has today. Our foreign critics admit that we have great wealth and abounding material prosperity; but our crime-record stares them in the face, and I am afraid that many of them are justified in feeling that we have not enough spirituality as a nation. True, we may say that our foreign critics also have very little spirituality; but the fact remains that an essential something is lacking in our country today, which is proved by our frightful inability to cope adequately with crime.

We have very many churches, we have fine institutions, we have splendid minds endeavoring to lift the burdens; but crimes of all kinds are increasing all the time; and so are our disappointments, our heartaches, our despair, and our misery.

With conditions as they are in the world today, I am glad that I have no children. What have we of great worth to offer to our children under the present condition of things? I tell you, it is a sad and pathetic picture.

We must bring ourselves to the point where we dare to examine ourselves.

I know that man has a heritage that is glorious and magnificent in power of possible service. When a man looks away from himself he gains a clear vision, and is moved by a quality of compassion that takes every suffering human being into his heart. He does not condemn others; neither does he pass judgment on them. Instead, he spends his time in purifying his own life, in seeking the right path, and in finding the light. Having found it, he holds on to it with a stedfast resolution that also fills him with a conviction of the sacredness and the nobility of life. Once a man accentuates these qualities, which really represent the divine life in him, I do not believe that he could ever fall back.

Let us meet conditions in such a way that when tomorrow comes, we shall have the consciousness of having made a new record, that will be the result of the attitude of mind one is in when he says to himself: "I am determined," "I am resolved," "I dare to face the future," "I dare to meet life's issues, which heretofore my opinions and my notions have prevented me from understanding," "I dare to open the book of life, to study myself and to challenge all the weaknesses of my nature." In this lie wisdom and peace.

Such a true attitude of mind cannot fail you. It has not failed me, and it has not failed many.

No Self-Deception

As soon as we are sure of man's spirituality, another page in the book of Life is opened for us and we begin to find ourselves in a whirl of splendid efforts; and we then see that the questions which puzzled us yesterday and which we ignored, are now right at hand ready to be looked into and solved.

A resolution supported by the spiritual will is of a magnificent and sacred quality. Such a resolution promises a great and superb future for man, if he will only move away from his weaknesses and abominate them as he would the ravages of some terrible disease.

Under the Higher Law there can be no self-deception. Man must treat himself as a being too sacred to be soiled or spoiled or bemeaned. He must hold himself with thought, will, and vision, to a new quality of dignity which never comes from the mentality alone.

Theosophists are trying to enlighten the mind of man so that he will be unafraid of himself, and so that he will realize that in his own nature there are the two qualities that will either make his life a blessing or mar it. Although he may carry the appearance of dignity and honor and decency, so long as there is one hidden weakness in his nature that he passes by or excuses or temporizes with, he is bemeaning himself, dragging himself down to inevitable degradation.

Theosophists realize that if we study ourselves honestly and begin the conquest of our own weaknesses we shall then have no time to condemn others. We have just as much as we can do to take care of ourselves, to discriminate at all times between right and wrong, between justice and injustice, between our personal limitations and the larger impersonal view of life. If we follow this path conscientiously we can arise each morning and meet the day with joy.

No matter what the difficulties that we may encounter at any time, we can meet them with courage, when we understand Theosophy; because we then know that man is essentially divine. This essential divinity shows itself by the way in which he lives his life, and by his living in harmony with the nobler aspects of life, thus fulfilling the decrees of the Higher Law. Every sane man at one time or another has high ideals and aspirations. The failures come when the personal will is not directed nor inspired by the spiritual nature.

The Place of Reason

One may think all day with mere brain-mind thoughts, and they will carry him only just so far; because one cannot find the peace and the joy of life nor the real explanations of life simply by reasoning. Reason is a great factor in our makeup, it is true; it must be educated and cultivated; but it is certainly not the sublime, central Fire in man.

The great spiritual message that is in the air today, which Theosophy brings once more to humanity, is that man is an inseparable part of the great eternal Scheme of Life; that as he applies the truths of right living to his daily conduct, and thus beautifies and purifies his own life, he feels his inner strength and realizes the glory of right living; he moves ever upward and onward in life after life, experience after experience, until he reaches a state which to us is relative perfection.

There is surely nothing irrational about such a philosophy! There are many thousands of people who a few years ago knew nothing about Theosophy, but who today are living in the joy of its discovery, and in the peace which this discovery brings. They have within themselves that quality of stedfast resolution that springs from the spiritual will. The key to it all is the belief in man's essential divinity.

Man must have this belief in his own essential divinity, in his power to make his life such that in time we shall see magnificent types of manhood and womanhood among us. Then we shall have children born in accordance with the divine scheme of things — born in purity, in virtue, and showing at least some of the strength of the spiritual will.

The greater things that we are to find,

that we must make active from day to day and from hour to hour, come from man's knowledge of his own inner nature. He must realize that it is the imperfections of the individual that bring to humanity its misery. He must face himself so honestly that he will say to himself: "I dare not meet the consequences that will come from my failures. I am no longer satisfied with my limitations, with my ignorance. I will aspire; I am resolved to make of my life a beautiful thing! I will become!"

Human Duality

I wish I had the power of the greatest artist to paint the picture of the two natures in man, the higher and the lower.

When I was a child, I was taught to look for His Satanic Majesty outside of myself, but since I was eight years of age, I have had different conceptions.

Theosophy is so reasonable and so true; it does not make me in my estimation any greater than any one else; but it does give me the power to know the right from the wrong in myself and to acknowledge that whatever weakness there is, as far as I am concerned, it is inside myself, in the undeveloped part of my nature, in those tendencies that I was born with, and that I inherited from generations past. So, as I have said before, I have no time to waste in condemning others.

The future is before us with its sublime possibilities. The spiritual laws are working all the time and have been active for untold millions and millions of years, on this plane and on all planes. When we understand this we shall have a larger vision of life, and a belief in the glory of the Universal ever living in man.

Every man has within him a divine ray, and it can be aroused. As long as he has that, he has the power to change his life in a moment, if he so will, and to look back upon all former mistakes as something pitiful and terrible, to be sure, but to be entirely shut out from the picture of the future, which is filled with golden hopes of the new life. The secret of making this change lies within himself.

Let us give to the sacredness of life its true value. Let us realize its spiritual beauty and its deeper intimacies with the Divine. Let us become so imbued with these larger views that we shall ourselves find peace and give peace to all others and thus change the whole aspect of the world for the better.

SECTION X

Here and There

To fulfil the law of our own being we must know our own essential Divinity and thus hold ourselves spiritually self-centered, ever living in a higher state of consciousness.

ON LOMALAND'S PERENNIAL CHARMS

*Point Loma, California,
June, 1927.*

ALL days are lovely here in our beautiful California, even when we have the soft, gray days. They all seem to have a special meaning. . . .

Our gardens are filled with flowers and our rooms carry the perfume of the same all through the days. And we never had so many birds as this year. They are the dearest things; they prattle and sing away as though they had just come home after being away in a cold storm somewhere. They come to our windows in such a friendly way, as though they remembered us. . . .

Let me tell you that when we look out on the wonderful trees and the beautiful flowers that grow on this Hill, we can see a dream of beauty and grandeur and real inspiration; but if we should set about trying to look up the things that we did not like, our mind would be so filled with the disagreeable images of our own creation that we could not see the beautiful things that everybody else sees. We should probably see only the faded flowers in the garden, the dead branches on the trees, withered leaves and broken limbs, or some other imperfection of Nature that one can always find if that is what he is looking for.

But the cause of it all would be that *our minds would be twisted*. For you know, "Two things cannot occupy the same place at the same time."

*Point Loma, California,
July, 1927.*

NATURE is indeed bountiful here. The flowers and the birds and the sweet pure air of Lomaland, and the gladness of the children, and the hopes and services of the members, all go to make life unique and splendid for us all.

The climate here is more glorious than

you can imagine. In December the flowers are in bloom, the birds are singing, and the trees are spreading their beautiful coloring through the atmosphere, and the grass is growing and our rich fruits have come, and we have the benefits of them, to bring us back to health.

Point Loma is a dream of beauty. It is said to be a paradise. The trees have grown up beyond the roofs of the houses, and our grounds are covered also with flowers and shrubbery and new buildings. . . .

If I had not had Theosophy all these years, I would have left this world long ago. The deception, the insincerity, and the rottenness in so many people who stand in the world as 'all right,' and who pass for good friends, have shocked me so that I have turned away from doing anything in the world but to work out these great problems of Theosophy, which I love, in order that people may from them receive the inspiration and the help and the knowledge that will make life worth living. It is causes that interest me.

Thank the gods! While the whole world may desert me, I shall have that abiding knowledge and faith that there is another life, and then another, and then others, and that love is eternal; and once it opens itself out into the service of humanity, it does not stop.

What the future has in store, I do not know. But I do the best I can. I have a supreme faith in the Higher Law; and I keep my conscience clear and do my full duty by those whom I meet as well as by myself, and particularly so with members. So I must pull through. . . .

ON "MOTHERS' DAY"

MOTHERS' DAY — a very grand day, I think, because it appeals to the better side of our natures; and wherever it is considered in the sacred sense in which we should consider it, it must bring out grand and splendid results in the hearts of the people.

So many beautiful and exquisite thoughts come up in connexion with Mothers' Day, that I know it is alive with high purposes. I have been wishing that we had Mothers' Day every day, and that we had had it all down the ages, so that the condition of the world might prove that mother had never been forgotten!

Limited as mothers' education must have been in comparison with what it will be, still all that we love, the best and noblest, was evoked in their motherhood.

It is not enough to think of their virtues and the beautiful things that have been done by them; but if we reflect a little, we can pay tribute to them by remembering the things that have not been done for them — the opportunities that have been denied them, the education which should have been theirs, in order that they might have lived out the fuller, richer, and grander aspirations of their souls. They should have been freed ages ago from that terrible idea, against which I speak every Sunday, about being 'born in sin'— they and their children! They should have had no fear, no anxiety, no sorrow; for the mother's life is very holy, very beautiful; and if it is sanctified with high purposes and unselfish work, it blesses succeeding ages.

Greater things — deeper wisdom, more profound knowledge of life and its meaning — must be ours as a people, if we are to pass on to posterity something that will live and become an enlightening power for humanity. It is the very lack of these enlightening and spiritual teachings, which should have been ours, that has prevented us from attaining real civilization.

It is wonderful how well mothers have done without them. But oh! how much grander, how much better, how much more wonderful a civilization we should have today — one that we could really pride ourselves on — if our dear mothers, with their sorrows and their heartaches and their anxieties, could have been freed from all the fetters of ignorance and of false teachings that hold down the minds of the people!

So I hold that the greatest tribute that

we can pay to mothers today is to try to establish in the minds of the people — even of the indifferent, the careless, the half-hearted, and the ungrateful — something of the spirit that comes from a knowledge that man is divine in essence, that he has the power to shape his life for glorious achievements. That is what we must awaken in the minds of all.

This day must not be one of tribute and dedication only; but everyone must be filled with a new idea of a better posterity, a better condition of human life. It is time that the united people of our country, or at any rate the united force of a few, should sweep away the horrible things that we have to meet from day to day.

I should feel ill at ease if I went to bed tonight with the thought that I had spent my time in paying merely verbal tribute to the mothers. Let us pay tribute to them, of course; but let us do something more! Let us honor them so truly that we give something worth while to pass on to those who follow after them! To the mothers with us now, I say that they may find within the teachings of Theosophy those fundamental principles and forces that can make one over again. Theosophy brings new hope, new joy; it gives a new vista of life.

ON WHITE LOTUS DAY

THIS day is very sacred to Theosophists. Our members all over the world celebrate today as "White Lotus Day"— the anniversary of the passing away in London, on May 8, 1891, of Helena Petrovna Blavatsky, the Foundress of the modern Theosophical Movement.

Perhaps in a few hundred years, H. P. Blavatsky will be universally recognised as the very remarkable character that Theosophists now know her to have been.

She possessed rare qualities of unselfish devotion to humanity. If she had held in abeyance some of the superb enthusiasm that was hers, she might not have been so much misunderstood. If she had kept back some of the glorious teachings of the Ancient Wisdom, which she brought again to the western world, possibly a great many more would have at least half-believed in her.

But she was imbued with a force of character that knew no limit and that marked her from the time we first knew her until she passed away, as a friend of the people — a soulful character, who moved out from a home of princely affluence and great prestige in Russia, with everything at her command in the worldly sense; all of which she gave up for a great purpose — to teach Theosophy.

She must have sought for Theosophy far and wide in lives before this incarnation, and have mastered the spiritual and intellectual import of many languages, sciences, religions, and philosophies; and thus having found Theosophy — 'Divine Wisdom'— her great purpose was to reach the hearts of the people with its message. She traveled through many different countries, in this life, sowing the seeds of brotherhood and of all the wonderful doctrines that are found in the teachings of Theosophy.

But from the beginning of her public work until the end, she was outrageously abused. Nevertheless she worked incessantly, sowing the seeds of brotherhood wherever she went; and she wrote her books that are the marvel of the age. Even today the greatest savants are baffled when they read her *Secret Doctrine* and her *Isis Unveiled*. The depth of her knowledge and the scope of her spiritual erudition are staggering.

The whole beauty of her character lay in the nobility of her high purposes. She had grand principles to support her in the teachings of Theosophy, which she inculcated into the minds of people all over the world, and the influence of her life-work is growing more and more rapidly all the time.

To pay adequate tribute to her in words is utterly impossible. But in the silence of our hearts, we Theosophists here and throughout the world, today are rejoicing in the thought that such a soul came to the world in our time, and that her work is a living power in the life of humanity, and that we have the privilege of participating in it.

And that is the greatest tribute we can pay to her; for no language can describe our admiration for her and our confidence in her mission, and the inspiration we have received from all that she said and did.

ON OPTIMISM

To an old Friend afflicted with ill Health and Discouragement

IN your letter you say: "All memories are tinged with sadness." I agree with you that most of them are, but *not all* of them; and the very fact that most of them are tinged with sadness *makes me doubly appreciate those that are not*. If we did not have the contrasts, we should become so used to having everything as we wanted it that we should not appreciate our very best memories. So keep a cheerful thought! In that way we won't be led to do something foolish and throw ourselves off the track.

You say, "The present is unendurable and the future utterly hopeless." I won't have it, because I know better! It is no miracle, and it requires no great marvelous effort. Oh! if you would take one whole day and claim it as your own, and swear by the eternal gods, no matter how many aches or pains you have, no matter how much disappointment you have, you are going to make of the day something that will bring you contentment — Peace!

Of course, in doing this, you would have to give up some of your notions; because you have absolutely got notions. Your notion is that you are depressed, and that your nerves are all gone. And then you fail, instead of trusting in the power of those invisible and higher laws that do help us when we help ourselves.

You see, I know you have made many

splendid efforts in your life; but you have not in this case made a bit of effort to pull yourself out of the idea that "the mind is so incomprehensible."

And then you say: "I conclude that man is a machine, that every thought and action is the result of outside influences." I will not admit that a man is a machine. No! The mind is an instrument of power and ability, if a man will trust his own inner nature and have the courage to meet his weaknesses and overcome them!

You continue: "Every thought and action is the result of outside influences, the impressions of what you see, what you hear, what you run up against!" Yes, if you become receptive and ready to let them run up against you. But we must be ready to defend that which is ourselves — our soul's rights, our opportunities, our honor, and our happiness! We have to be on the defensive; this gives us strength.

You say further: "Each affects the mind and therefore the mind has to work exactly as it does . . . according to the laws given to the machine." Yes, it does, just as long as you let it. But why open the doors to those things that do not belong to you, that you do not want? Why not remove fear, and doubt, and swear there will be a few days in your life that shall tell for something akin to your aspirations and your ideals? You cannot formulate them; but you can go into the spirit of something new. And if you were with me, I would pull you out of your present depressed state of mind.

And then again, you are away off the track when you say: "We have but little, if any responsibility." Why, ——, it is just the other way! It is not until one begins to find that he is responsible, that he pulls out of his moods, and doubts, and questionings, etc. And it is no hard fight at all! I have found that every effort made in that line by me doubles my power to help those I know, and I grow spiritually also.

If we are going to let the mere nature-forces run a man, we shall have the lower part of his nature, his weaknesses, and his doubts, all the time mingling in with his aspirations. Oh, your attitude is pathetic, and I am not going to allow it!

There is something amusingly contradictory in your letter; for, in spite of all these things that you say at the beginning, which I have referred to, you say: "But we must all try to improve the future." But my dear ——, you are putting your future too far away from you. Improve the *now;* improve the day all by yourself in your thought!

Seek the sunshine in your thoughts! Do not allow the suggestion of a thought to remain with you that will make any shadows, nor anything that will make you unhappy. I tell you that life lived aright, is joy! Just play a part! Be an actor for a while; and see what will come of it. Thus may you find yourself.

ON THE IMMORTALITY OF GENIUS

To the Bereaved Sister of a great Artist

YOU have my fullest sympathy in the loss of your dear brother. But remember, that that which you loved most in him is immortal and can never die! And then think what a beautiful memory of himself he has left for all time in his lovely paintings.

Do believe me, dear, your brother is still close to you in essence, though not in form, because the latter would be retrogression instead of advancement for the soul, and Theosophy does not teach that. But love is eternal, and his highest thoughts are probably close to you now, and his hopes and his wishes, unmarred by the brain-mind and the flesh-life. Believe in it and trust in it!

In his present soul-existence, he goes on painting his beautiful pictures, because the soul is living in the glory of what it accomplished here in this life and further creation.

If he had known the secrets of preserving his health, he might have been with us today. He will be wiser in the next incarnation. Have trust, dear, in the wonderful, optimistic teachings of Theosophy!

ON "THE LIFE OF PYTHAGORAS"

By Iamblichus

(Thomas Taylor's translation)

WELL worth reading; brim full of the sweet gems of thought and spiritual hints that give one new knowledge every time he reads a line.

Pythagoras was most truly a great Mystic, and the simplicity of his life reminds me very much of Judge's. Both were very spiritual men, born at different times, under different conditions; but their light still shines, and their books will be read by thousands and thousands in the future.

ON "LETTERS FROM A CHINESE OFFICIAL"

I HAVE read three times a little book entitled, *Letters from a Chinese Official: Being an Eastern View of Western Civilization;* and am going to read it again.

How I do admire the writer! How clear-sighted he is! How unbiased! How true! How far-visioned! Awfully clever, he was too, to write what he knew was the truth, and at the same time prevent any possibility of his being misunderstood by political intriguers to the detriment of China. He so wisely 'knocked into smithereens' so many things that are unnecessary in the human life of the Western World!

ON COLONEL CHARLES A. LINDBERGH

MY thoughts turn to young Lindbergh, the aviator. Somewhere along the way, it will be found that he marked time with a positive quality of his nature that brought the spirit of self-control; and that self-control has marked the history of his whole life in very small things; so that when his hands were guiding his aeroplane all that long distance from New York to Paris, the revelation came to him of the lessons he had learned, and the conquests he had made from childhood.

Then the power and majesty of soul, which had given its enlightenment in small ways — in devotion to duty, in real honesty, and great conscientiousness,— enabled him to become the controller of his destiny, and to win the honor of the best in the world.

Great lessons can be learned from studying the life of this young man.

When we all come to the point where we are absolutely honest with ourselves, with not a bit of anything false in us, we also shall make our mark, a high mark that cannot be dreamed of yet.

In this new-born time, new opportunities are ours, if we will take them. And they are nearer to us, because of what this young Lindbergh has achieved in his simple, heroic effort and in his self-control as a man.

. . . . .

I THINK that there is something behind Lindbergh's coming out as he did. I believe in the guidance of the Real Teachers, and there is much that could be said.

I think time will prove that internationally the thought-world in a sense has been vastly changed through the splendid way he conducted himself in his daring international venture. It is a stimulus and may set some weaklings to turn about and try to do better and make the world more glad.

TO A CONSCIENTIOUS MOTHER

KEEP young people ever pushing forward! Let them feel that they have to work for ever higher achievements; that they can make mistakes, and that they should always be ready to be guided and directed in the right way. If you let a child feel that it can do everything that it wishes, or that it is close to perfection, she will not strive much in the direction of improvement and growth; and then when trouble comes, she is not ready.

I pray that you may have no disappointments, no heartaches; but I know that, being such a thoughtful mother, you are looking well ahead and are helping your daughter to find her strength, which comes not just from her brain-mind, and not just from what she accomplishes that is in a general way satisfactory, but from that part of her nature which rounds out her character from the spiritual side of her being, and makes her true — true to herself all the time.

ON FRIENDSHIP

WHAT a beautiful thing is a dear, noble, unselfish friendship! It makes one forget so many disappointments and heartaches, and it makes one feel more sure of the great value, inspiration, and protection that the Higher Law affords us, when we work with it.

ON INNER PEACE

THERE is an inner peace that one can find that is the keynote of one's life. It opens the inner possibilities of one's heart; makes one become more receptive to his higher thoughts; and it holds one enthroned, so to speak, in strength.

LIGHT FROM THE MOUNTAIN-TOPS

STICK to your place; hold to your duty; do it fully; keep the conscience clean; live in the sunshine of the eternal things, and all good things whatsoever will come to you!

Our Work goes along splendidly, and I

have evidence of the silent assistance that comes when I have done my best. It is great that the radiant light of Truth is ever near, if we can bend our heads and listen in silence. It is joy unspeakable, and keeps one ever climbing. A great idea that of climbing!

Well, the ball keeps rolling, rolling; the dear old Masters are tramping along the great pathway, and the Light shines forth in resplendent glory from the mountain-tops, where the eyes of most men fail to glimpse it.

"THE CARAVAN MOVES ON"

HOW quickly the time passes when one's mind is occupied in such stupendous efforts for the benefit of *the human race: and how much sorrow passes us by, with simply a nod, because we are not on the road of worry and anxiety and selfishness!*

The different states of mind that men have are very puzzling; and only those who move out of the limitations of these states of mind, can tell of the grandeur of the growth of the inner life.

It is surely a joy to live and work for these great, these noble purposes, which have fascinated thousands and thousands of pilgrims along the way through aeons of time. The Great Caravan moves on, and we are in the march.

There is music in the air, there is joy in the heart; and so we salute the day as our day, the winning day, because we can perpetuate the glorious life and thoughts of H. P. Blavatsky and William Q. Judge.

ON SELF-CONFIDENCE AND COURAGE

To a young Aspirant

CERTAINLY you are on the right road to find the light. But this light cannot come from me nor from any other than yourself. It will spring from your heart, out of the yearnings of your soul for better things.

If people would only take up their burdens with a courage that acknowledges no defeat, life would be very different. Such courage gives one a royal soul-optimism. This in turn gives one confidence in oneself. And self-confidence strikes a deeper note in the life — a spiritual note, an inspiring note,— whereby the soul can rise and go out in thought into the larger realms of being, and therein find that peace which passeth all understanding. . . .

Here is one little hint that I can give you to make your path easier: Live each day as though it were your last. In other words, make up your mind that each day shall be filled with an undeniable record of your devotion to truth and to principle. Let each day prove that you appreciate the value of time to such extent that you only do those things that tell for good and that you set behind you all temptations to draw you away from the path you have chosen.

ON THE UNIVERSAL BROTHERHOOD AND THEOSOPHICAL SOCIETY

THERE is nothing in the Universal Brotherhood and Theosophical Society that unselfish, aspiring, intelligent people could object to. The selfish and the ambitious might object to the management of the Organization being left entirely in the hands of the Leader and Official Head, by our constitution; but the oldest members of our Society, as well as the most active and intelligent among the younger members, appreciate the fact that only so can the unity of the whole be preserved and the teachings be kept pure and undefiled, and the Organization be saved from exploitation by the unworthy.

All the Sages of the past knew and most thoughtful people of today realize that it is safer in a spiritual movement to have power centralized in the hands of one person of true character to guide the affairs and the policy of the Organization along the right path, and to preserve harmony. The very teachings of Theosophy themselves are a guarantee against dogmatism and bigotry.

Once the people acknowledge to themselves this self-evident fact, I am sure they will individually seek the protection and the real spirit of Brotherhood afforded by membership in our Society, which is established on a solid foundation and is destined to an ever-widening influence in the world for the good of all humanity.

ON THE SACRED OBLIGATIONS OF A THEOSOPHIST

I AM thinking of H. P. Blavatsky and William Q. Judge — in their experiences, their struggles, their great efforts, and also in all their victories; for their victories were many. But the world knew not of them and could not have comprehended them, even if it had known them.

And then I thought of the great changes

that have been wrought in the interval of time since H. P. Blavatsky was bending her energy and her soul-effort to enlighten the public of America, and since dear William Q. Judge was working along in his great Theosophical efforts.

Of course those who belong to the old days will recall the desperate efforts that were made by our opponents from the very beginning to crush out all possibility of Theosophy becoming a living power in the lives of the people of the world. Few will know how many schemes were made and carried out to make impossible the work of establishing the Theosophical Society in America.

When we go back in thought, during our quiet moments, we must recall struggle after struggle that H. P. Blavatsky had and that Mr. Judge had in their own inner lives, while waiting for the results of their grand efforts.

But there is a great charm about Theosophical study. Once the mind is conscious that the spiritual soul exists, there is a superb companionship through all the struggles and de-

OBLIGATIONS OF A THEOSOPHIST

feats as well as all the successes and victories; and, above all, in the visions for the future. So those two people in everything that they experienced had ever before them the vision of the future of Theosophy for the whole world, and we have already begun to glimpse it.

Think what these two people were doing in carrying out this great unselfish effort to lift humanity's burdens — in the beginning, practically alone! Suppose they had failed! Suppose they had carried out their wishes rather than their duties, where would we be today and where would Theosophy be today? And where could we find a promise for the future of humanity?

In these thoughts there is a great lesson. No man, no woman, no Theosophist, knows how far his influence goes in ingraining into the thought-atmosphere of the world these beautiful teachings. One cannot tell how far they will go.

It is difficult to think towards any one of the principles of the Theosophical teachings without feeling new life, and new hope, and new determination, and the will strengthened through the efforts and application of one's mind to self-improvement and to the service of humanity.

In marking time with the age, and, indeed, in stepping out ahead of it, one has to be well acquainted with oneself; one must be at home with oneself; one must have respect for oneself; one must have trust in oneself. And this cannot come without a recognition of the essential divinity of man.

Step by step we can trace the growth of the Universal Brotherhood and Theosophical Society and point out how much has been accomplished by this one woman from Russia, when she came to the western world; but no matter how much we may think of it, every day in the year, we cannot approximate what she wanted to do, or what she did do, or what she meant that we should do. She enfolded in her arms, so to speak, the great universal family of the world. Why? Because her vision was so large, and her soul told her that all she had to do was day by day to follow her duty, do her noble service, forget herself in that service; and from that would come the superb strength that brought her to victory, preserved this Society, and gave us the grand opportunity and satisfaction that are ours in having established and maintained this World's Center of Theosophy at Point Loma.

With the help of Mr. Judge she carried the Society on; so that on inner planes it is really marvelous how much was done in the early days.

According to the laws of Occultism, as I understand them, when our thoughts are ingrained into the atmosphere where we are carrying on our Theosophical work, when our purposes are true and our wills are behind them, there is no limitation to the power of even one individual effort.

So when one thinks of the combined efforts of the body of people that we have at Point Loma now and of the members throughout the world all working together, it seems almost impossible to think how great the transition has been in the short space of thirty years and how wonderful the advancement of the Theosophical Movement that has been made since the time when H. P. Blavatsky stood here in this country alone and persecuted. Look where our work stands now before the world!

But we must not stop here. We must have prevision; we must extend our souls' vision out so far that, while we keep on in the performance of our daily duties, we can concentrate our thoughts on the superb possibilities of the future — not only on the possibilities of the members of this Society, but on those of the whole world.

If every student had done his full duty to the full extent of the knowledge of Theosophy that was his, to this date, we should have tens of thousands of members for every hundred that we have today; and our whole great Theosophical body would have been farther advanced, because there would have been a stronger unity and a more profound expression of the real Theosophical life throughout.

OBLIGATIONS OF A THEOSOPHIST 301

So, while we are doing very well, and while we are doing better perhaps than many of us ever thought we could do, we are still doing so very little in comparison with what we may do. But this is where we must stand. If we dare to look backward or to throw our thoughts on to ourselves as to our own inability and say to ourselves: "I cannot," or "I will not," or "I want," and allow ourselves to wander on to the path of desire, we lose our way; and we know not how much we lose. In just dropping the mind for five minutes into a support of the wrong side of one's nature, one does not know how much will creep in; one does not know how much harm is done, nor how much these small doings may lead to greater wrong.

Not until we can brighten our minds with the more divine thoughts, until we can enliven our beings with a determination to make the spiritual life a glorious reality within us, shall we find our true places in the Divine Scheme.

If we truly serve the Cause of Theosophy, depend upon it and serve it fully, all else goes well. But if in our mental limitations we shy off from our duty and slip into this mood and that mood, or this desire and that desire, remember we shall have to go over the same ground again, and perhaps not under such favorable circumstances; because there is always a lesson — a lesson that only the soul or the mind can comprehend, that cannot be talked about, but that is made evident whenever there is even a half-failure, when there is the play of the two forces in the nature.

Oh, the tremendous egoism that exists today, alas! even with some of our so-called Theosophists! They have it to a very remarkable degree sometimes. In their own estimation they are in a position to judge all others as to their Theosophical attitude. Such egoists cannot be taught anything. They go along with their heads set high and with an air of impressing their own importance upon their fellows as the greatest and grandest type of woman or man. When such egoism is controlling the life, if one could see on inner planes, one would see clouds, one would see smoke, one would see discouragement and despair. Then comes pity and then come tears because it is so.

Returning to my picture of H. P. Blavatsky and William Q. Judge, I feel that they are both rejoicing with us; and that in their hearts is something that overrides any thought of what their approbation would be. Knowing that they loved us so well, I think they would say even more than I have said: that we cannot stand still for a moment. We must not be satisfied with just one stride we make for the day; but that stride, or that effort, or that devotion, or that concentration, must be vivified with the real spiritual vitality of soul-action.

So I refer very often to the sacredness of duty, and the sacredness of our opportunities, and the profound sacredness of our obligations as honest and devoted Theosophists.

ON THE VALUE OF TIME AND THEOSOPHICAL RESPONSIBILITIES

THE feeling of the value of time, and of the responsibilities that are ours in our Theosophical efforts, takes us quite away from the everyday forces of life, away from personal ends, and carries us out into a realm of thought that is so universal and so alive with possibilities that we find ourselves in a new world, a world of greater effort, of sublime effort, for the advancement of the human race.

Let us consider for a moment the subject 'Why not Cultivate the Real Man and Woman instead of the Artificial?' When one thinks of and takes up these larger subjects, when one gives the right thought towards the meaning of each life and of the great creative forces that are back of each life, then one realizes that — aside from Theosophy — we know nothing about all these wonderful things. We cannot otherwise tell whence come these great forces into our individual lives every day, waiting for us to utilize them; and we stand or move along trying to do something; but we do not do it richly and fully and understandingly enough.

We ought to count ourselves as very important factors in the universe. We should look upon ourselves as spiritual beings in preparation for a glorious work that the world has not known for ages; and we are trying to revivify and to resuscitate those ancient teachings that were so sacred and so sublime of old. They have lived in the silence and in the memories of the great workers and of the great Teachers; they have lived in the inner life of the great men all through the ages.

But if H. P. Blavatsky and William Q. Judge had not come here and done their great work, these teachings would not have been given to the outer world.

Challenge yourselves every night and every morning, as you challenge the glory of the sun in the morning and the gladness of the day! Carry out the great idea of the opportunities that you have of being real heralders, real protectors, of this Sacred Work, of which if even one failed, possibly the whole would be lost.

You are challenged; and the beauty of it is that you want to be. We all must desire to be challenged; we must rejoice in the thought that we have the opportunity to declare the sublimity of life and the joy of life, and the divine influence of Theosophy. It grows more beautiful every day.

The larger your vision, the broader your field of work, the more determined and the more strenuous you are, the nearer do these richer opportunities come, and the nearer comes the knowledge of your essential divinity.

A HEART-MESSAGE

TO THE LITTLE FOLK ALL OVER THE WORLD

Lomaland, December 18, 1927.

DEAR CHILDREN: Christmas will soon be here and we are all in good cheer. Even the birds are singing a glad song of the happy time of Christmas. If the birds can sing and the flowers can smile and love so well, why cannot the little folk all join now in being the most gladsome of all that lives?

Little girls and boys should have their minds pure and clean. Then they would always be happy, and jolly, and glad. They should live in the sunshine and love the flowers and sing as the birds sing, and join in the glad time of Christmas; and never lose their tempers or be naughty or untruthful or insincere.

All the little children throughout the world, feeling these beautiful thoughts and wishing to make this year the happiest year of their lives, are singing the one great song of a happy, merry Christmas.

So, dear children, I who love all the little boys and girls everywhere, and who have many Lotus-Children in different countries, join with you in saying: "A Merry Christmas! A Merry Christmas! A Merry Christmas to you, to Father and Mother and all the family, and to all the world!"

And, above everything, let us remember all the little children who have not as much comfort and happiness as we have — many who are suffering and lying sick in the hospitals or crippled or injured. It is they whom we must think of. We must not make Christmas a selfish day, but an unselfish day, a glad day, a love-day. Then these unhappy children will read your hearts and know your loving thoughts.

Good-bye! Salutations to you and to your dear teachers!

    Affectionately,
      KATHERINE TINGLEY.

STANDARD THEOSOPHICAL LITERATURE

published or for sale by the
THEOSOPHICAL PUBLISHING COMPANY
a department of the
UNIVERSAL BROTHERHOOD AND THEOSOPHICAL SOCIETY
Point Loma, California
UNDER THE LEADERSHIP OF KATHERINE TINGLEY

THE SECRET DOCTRINE: *The Synthesis of Science, Religion, and Philosophy,* by H. P. Blavatsky. Virtually a verbatim reprint of the original edition published in 1888 by by H. P. Blavatsky   per set

    2 vols., in 4 parts (limp)   12.00
    2 vols., in 2 parts (fabr.)   10.00

ISIS UNVEILED: *A Master-Key to the Mysteries of Ancient and Modern Science and Theology,* by H. P. Blavatsky   (4 vols.)   per set   12.00

THE KEY TO THEOSOPHY: *A Clear Exposition, in the Form of Question and Answer, of the Ethics, Science, and Philosophy, for the Study of which The Universal Brotherhood and Theosophical Society has been founded, with a copious Glossary of General Theosophical Terms,* by H. P. Blavatsky   per copy   2.25

THEOSOPHY: THE PATH OF THE MYSTIC: per copy
  A unique collection of Citations gilt edge 3.25
  from the Teachings of Katherine gift 2.50
  Tingley, including extracts from fabrikoid 1.25
  Private Instructions paper .75

THE WINE OF LIFE: *The Wisdom of sane mysticism presented with a beauty of diction and wealth of illustration unsurpassed. An inspiration for the daily life of the individual, home, nation, and humanity*, by Katherine Tingley. Special Autograph leather
  per copy
  3.00
  5.00

THE GODS AWAIT: *A lucid exposition of the higher philosophy of life; fragrant with the aroma of spirituality*, by Katherine Tingley
  per copy
  2.00

THE TRAVAIL OF THE SOUL: *Old wisdom in twentieth-century language. Profound truths simply put*, by Katherine Tingley
  per copy
  2.00

THE VOICE OF THE SOUL: *Setting forth in beautiful language the part played by man's spiritual nature in the drama of life*, by Katherine Tingley
  per copy
  2.00

BHAGAVAD-GÎTÂ: *The Book of Devotion. A Dialog between Krishna, Lord of Devotion, and Arjuna, Prince of India. An Episode from the Mahâbhârata, India's Great Epic. Recension* by W. Q. Judge
  per copy
  1.00

THE VOICE OF THE SILENCE, and other fragments from the *Book of the Golden Precepts*. Dedicated to the Few. Translated and Annotated by H. P. Blavatsky   per copy .75

THE OCEAN OF THEOSOPHY: *A Statement of fundamental truths made in such a manner as to be understandable by the ordinary reader*, by William Q. Judge   per copy cloth 1.00 paper .75

ECHOES FROM THE ORIENT: *A Broad Outline of Theosophical Doctrine*, by William Quan Judge   per copy cloth .50 paper .25

REINCARNATION: A STUDY OF FORGOTTEN TRUTH, by E. D. Walker. A work valuable alike to the student of Theosophy and to the general reader. Point Loma ed.   per copy (cloth) 1.75

HELENA PETROVNA BLAVATSKY, by Katherine Tingley: with Quotations from the writings of H. P. Blavatsky; tributes by W. Q. Judge and Students   per copy cloth .90 paper .75

A NOSEGAY OF EVERLASTINGS: *from Katherine Tingley's Garden of Helpful Thoughts.* Short extracts culled from various addresses delivered in Europe and America   per copy cloth .75 paper .50

OM: THE SECRET OF AHBOR VALLEY: *Profound truths in the guise of vivid and fascinating fiction, by one of the most prominent writers of today*. A novel by Talbot Mundy — per copy .75

THE SECRET MOUNTAIN: *Mystical stories, told with true poetical imagination*, by Kenneth Morris — per copy 2.00

THE FATES OF THE PRINCES OF DYFED: *A Romance from that Wonderland of Celtic Mythology of which so many literary exponents have won fame in the last thirty years: derived, however, from Welsh and not, as the mass of Neo-Celtic literature has been, from Irish sources*, by Cenydd Morus — per copy 2.00

THE PLOUGH AND THE CROSS: *A Story of New Ireland*, by Wm. Patrick O'Ryan — per copy 1.00

A NOSEGAY OF 'YORICK'S' EDITORIALS: *Compiled by a Student of Theosophical University, in memory of Edwin H. Clough, America's Great Journalist and Critic* — per copy .25

LOMALAND: An Album of Views of the International Headquarters at Point Loma, and Quotations from the three Theosophical Leaders (10 x 13 in., post. 6c. extra) — per copy .50

KATHERINE TINGLEY ON MARRIAGE AND THE HOME, by Claire Merton — per copy .25

CLASSICAL DRAMA SERIES: SOUVENIR ALBUM NO. 1 — *The Eumenides*. Beautiful half-tones of scenes from Aeschylus' Drama, as presented by Katherine Tingley in the Greek Theater; other pictures of topical interest; and an essay on "The Eumenides" by J. H. Fussell (48 pp. 9 x 12)   per copy 1.00

THEOSOPHICAL PAMPHLETS: 15c. per copy

AN EPITOME OF THEOSOPHY, by William Quan Judge

THE MYSTICAL CHRIST, by Katherine Tingley

THE READJUSTMENT OF THE HUMAN RACE THROUGH THEOSOPHY, by Katherine Tingley

DEATH, THE TWIN-SISTER OF LIFE, by Katherine Tingley

KATHERINE TINGLEY AND HER RÂJA-YOGA SYSTEM OF EDUCATION, by Lilian Whiting

KATHERINE TINGLEY: THEOSOPHIST AND HUMANITARIAN, by Lilian Whiting

SOME OF THE ERRORS OF CHRISTIAN SCIENCE, by H. P. Blavatsky and W. Q. Judge

THE EVILS OF HYPNOTISM, by Lydia Ross, M. D.

THEOSOPHY AND OCCULTISM. A Reply to M. Jules Bois, by J. H. Fussell

ON VERSE, "FREE VERSE," AND THE DUAL NATURE OF MAN, by Kenneth Morris

THEOSOPHICAL MANUALS

HANDBOOKS FOR STUDENTS

Per set (19 vols.), paper $4.00; cloth $5.50
paper .25; cloth .35 per copy

- No. 1. Elementary Theosophy
- No. 2. The Seven Principles of Man
- No. 3. Karma
- No. 4. Reincarnation
- No. 5. Man after Death
- No. 6. Kâma-loka and Devachan
- No. 7. Teachers and Their Disciples
- No. 8. The Doctrine of Cycles
- No. 9. Psychism, Ghostology, and the Astral Plane
- No. 10. The Astral Light
- No. 11. Psychometry, Clairvoyance, and Thought-Transference
- No. 12. The Angel and the Demon, 2 vols., 35c. each
- No. 13. The Flame and the Clay
- No. 14. On God and Prayer
- No. 15. Theosophy: the Mother of Religions
- No. 16. From Crypt to Pronaos: An Essay on the Rise and Fall of Dogma
- No. 17. Earth: Its Parentage, its Rounds and its Races
- No. 18. Sons of the Fire-Mist: A Study of Man

NEW CENTURY SERIES

THE PITH AND MARROW OF SOME SACRED WRITINGS

25c. per copy

SCRIPT 1 — *Contents:* The Relation of Universal Brotherhood to Christianity — No Man can Serve Two Masters — In this Place is a Greater Thing

SCRIPT 2 — *Contents:* A Vision of Judgment — The Great Victory — Co-Heirs with Christ — The 'Woes' of the Prophets — Fragment: from the *Bhagavad-Gîtâ* — Jesus the Man

SCRIPT 3 — *Contents:* Lesson of Israel's History — Man's Divinity and Perfectibility — The Man Born Blind — The Everlasting Covenant — Burden of the Lord

SCRIPT 4 — *Contents:* Reincarnation in the Bible — The Money-Changers in the Temple — The Mysteries of the Kingdom of Heaven — The Heart Doctrine — The Temple of God

SCRIPT 9 — *Contents:* Traces of the Wisdom-Religion in Zoroastrianism, Mithraism, and their modern representative, Parseeism — The Druses of Mount Lebanon

SCRIPT 10 — *Contents:* The Religions of China

SCRIPT 11 — *Contents:* Druidism — Druidism and its Connexion with Ireland

THE PATH SERIES

SPECIALLY ADAPTED FOR INQUIRERS IN THEOSOPHY
5c. per copy

No. 1. The Purpose of the Universal Brotherhood and Theosophical Society

No. 2. Theosophy Generally Stated (W. Q. Judge): *Reprinted from Official Report, World's Parliament of Religions, Chicago, 1893*

No. 3. Mislaid Mysteries (Herbert Coryn, M. D.)

No. 4. Theosophy and its Counterfeits

No. 5. Some Perverted Presentations of Theosophy (H. T. Edge, M. A.)

No. 6. What is Theosophy? (H. T. Edge, M. A.)

LOTUS LIBRARY FOR YOUNG FOLK

Introduced under the direction of Katherine Tingley

per copy

COMING OF THE KING, THE: by R. Machell (cloth) $.35

LITTLE BUILDERS, and their Voyage to Rangi, THE: by R. N. .50

LOTUS SONG: "*The Sun Temple,*" with music .15

LOTUS SONG BOOK. Fifty original songs with copyrighted music (boards) .50

LUZ STAR-EYE'S DREAM-JOURNEY TO THE ISLES OF THE SOUTHERN SEA. A Story for Children by YLVA. *Illustrations by the Author* (cloth) .75

STRANGE LITTLE GIRL, THE: A Story for Children, by V. M. *Illustrations by N. Roth* (cloth) .75

PAPERS OF THE SCHOOL OF ANTIQUITY

20c. per copy

No. 2. The Relation of Religion to Art in Antiquity and the Middle Ages: *by Osvald Sirén, Ph. D.*

No. 3. Notes on Peruvian Antiquities (*illustrated*): *by Fred. J. Dick, M. Inst. C. E.*

No. 8. Studies in Evolution: *by H. T. Edge, M. A.*

No. 9. The School of Antiquity: Its Meaning, Purpose, and Scope: *by J. H. Fussell*

No. 10. Problems in Ethnology: *by J. O. Kinnaman, A. M., Ph. D.*

No. 11. Neglected Fundamentals in Geometry: *by Fred. J. Dick, M. Inst. C. E.*

No. 13. Prehistoric Man and Darwinism: *by C. J. Ryan*

No. 12. Maya Chronology (*illustrated*): *by Fred. J. Dick, M. Inst. C. E.* — 2 parts 30c.

PERIODICALS

THE THEOSOPHICAL PATH (*illustrated, monthly*) Edited by Katherine Tingley
per copy, domestic .30; foreign .35 or 1s 6d.
per year $3.00; Canadian postage, .35; Foreign .50

PERIODICALS — *continued*

RÂJA-YOGA MESSENGER (*illustrated, bi-monthly*) Conducted by students of the Râja-Yoga College, under the direction of Katherine Tingley
per copy, domestic .20; foreign .25 or 1s.
per year $1.00; Canadian postage, .10; Foreign .20

THE NEW WAY (*illustrated, monthly*) Under the direction of Katherine Tingley: per copy .10
per year .75; Foreign $1.00

TRANSPORTATION CHARGES PREPAID

LITERATURE IN SWEDISH, DUTCH, GERMAN, FRENCH, SPANISH, ITALIAN and JAPANESE

FOREIGN AGENCIES

GREAT BRITAIN — Theosophical Book Co.,
 1 Bloomsbury St., LONDON, W. C. 1, ENGLAND

SWEDEN — Universella Broderskapets Förlag, Tegnérgatan 29, STOCKHOLM

HOLLAND — A. Goud, Tolsteegsingel 29, O. Z., UTRECHT

GERMANY — Dr. Hans Hackmann, Bayerischer Platz 12 BERLIN W. 30

AUSTRALIA — Box 1292 G. P. O., SYDNEY, N. S. W.

THE ARYAN THEOSOPHICAL PRESS
Point Loma, California

www.ingramcontent.com/pod-product-compliance
Lightning Source LLC
Chambersburg PA
CBHW030316100526
44592CB00010B/455